BAREFOOT
ON THE HILL
THE LIFE OF
HARRY HAYS

BAREFOOT
ON THE HILL
◆
THE LIFE OF
HARRY HAYS

DON PEACOCK

Douglas & McIntyre
Vancouver/Toronto

To Jean,
for reasons known to both of us.

Douglas & McIntyre Ltd., 1615 Venables Street, Vancouver, British Columbia V5L 2H1

Canadian Cataloguing in Publication Data

Peacock, Donald.
  Barefoot on the Hill

  Includes index.
  ISBN 0-88894-480-2

  1. Hays, Harry, 1909–1982. 2. Politicians –
  Canada – Biography. 3. Agriculturists –
Canada – Biography. 4. Cattle breeders –
Canada – Biography. I. Title.
FC621.H39P42 1986   971.064'092'4   C86-091219-1
F1034.3.H39P42 1986

Jacket photograph by Walter Petrigo
Jacket design by Barbara Hodgson
Design by Verna Wong
Typeset by Typeworks
Printed and bound in Canada by D. W. Friesen & Sons Ltd.

CONTENTS

PREFACE

Although we were both native Albertans, born outside but near Calgary, Harry Hays and I had never met until the day he interviewed me in his Parliament Hill office about my working for him as a special assistant.

Outwardly we might have seemed an unlikely political fit. In appearance and past experience, he typified the Parliament Hill sophisticated skeptic's stereotype of the staid western farmer—a short, stocky man in a plain brown suit who seemed uncomfortable wearing a white shirt and tie. At that time, I was the first reporter to represent a single privately owned radio station in the Parliamentary Press Gallery. With ten years' experience on the Hill, most with the Canadian Press, some with the *Financial Post,* my specialty then was covering Parliament in snappy thirty-second news reports for the Toronto rock station CHUM.

The title Special Assistant covers a multitude of possible activities on behalf of a cabinet minister, from none to handling their news media relations, preparing them for the Commons Question Period and writing their speeches. It can also include handling difficult demands from constituents, writing weekly newsletters for home-constituency voters' consumption and helping with the development of new policies. Another title for this kind of position is Backroom Political Hack. Today, in the light of advancing experience with various political processes, I prefer the second title and wear it, since the time I worked with Harry Hays, with pride.

In Hays's employ when he was Canada's minister of agriculture, I learned more in twenty-one months about how much more complexity, difficulty, tenacity and durability is demanded of our politicians than all my previous years as a parliamentary reporter had even hinted at—even though on the day of our initial interview, I considered myself a seasoned political observer. Watching the real thing, I first learned from working with Hays, is no substitute for being directly and personally involved in it. What I, together with Hays, also learned from experience, is that the chief purpose of democracy is not power alone but power used in the service of justice and equity, because a free society unremittingly demands this of its government. Hays, though disguised in a commonplace body, lived in a most uncommonplace soul and worked out of a most uncommonplace mind. The pleasure and stimulation of Hays's friendship and the achievements in agriculture and politics of his gifted intuition and intellect are what inspired the writing of this book.

This book could not have been written without the help of many other persons, as is true of any biographical account. I am not going to try to name all who have been of assistance because I know I will leave out some if I do, not out of a failure of appreciation but of memory.

I must, however, single out for special thanks Muriel, Harry Hays's wife, and Senator Dan Hays, his son, for their special help and co-operation. His brother Jack and sisters Catherine Watson, Laura Shaw and Virginia Reid were also generously open with their family recollections. Others who contributed valuable material include Senators H. A. ("Bud") Olson, Keith Davey and Ian Sinclair, former finance minister Walter Gordon, former prime minister Pierre Trudeau, Jean Chrétien, and Hays's many Alberta friends, among them Ed O'Connor, Charlie Kennedy, Marie Kennedy, Grant MacEwan, P. N. R. Morrison, Arthur Smith, Merv Anderson, Hays Ranches secretary Dianne Busko, CPR public relations archivists, certain unnamed Calgary city hall officials (then and now), and Doug Blair, to name the major names that come to mind. And not to forget J. Cameron Millikin and Robert Blair.

A special word of appreciation must be expressed to Suzanne Zwarun for invaluable help with interviews and to editor Ruth Fraser for the benignly ruthless enhancements of her implacable black pencil.

CHAPTER ONE

THE BUMPKIN FACTOR

During his brief, turbulent but productive adventure as Canadian minister of agriculture, Harry Hays sometimes deliberately played the part of gauche country boy caught barefoot on Parliament Hill. Although he never played the part seriously, he played it with serious purpose. At the time it seemed good politics for a lone Alberta Liberal tossing on a sea of rambunctious prairie Tories. And some folks, especially a few central Canadian city slickers in the news media, even believed this often amusing and occasionally outrageous image. But even the thickest of slickers caught on before too long that this was only one element in Hays's intuitive if unpolished talent for the political art.

A good reason why they caught on was given by one of his Tory predecessors in the Calgary South House of Commons seat Hays managed to win for the Liberals only once. Arthur Smith said of him after his death: "He was a much smarter man than most people gave him credit for. People often thought of Harry that he was just a country bumpkin, and you just got into a conversation with him for five minutes and you'd realize that he had really a very sharp mind."

This sharpness of mind, plus a love of initiating bold new ways in whatever work he was doing, helps to explain the unsung but lasting influence Hays had on Canadian, and even American and European, agriculture despite the brevity of his ministerial career. It also explains his lasting fascination with politics and government, to which he devoted the later decades of his life. This includes his final nationally prominent role as a co-chairman of the joint Commons-Senate Constitution committee. There, as a sort of last hurrah, he unwittingly ran afoul of the women's rights movement.

One of Canada's most famous journalist-authors, Peter C. Newman, dealt passingly with Hays early in his career. Newman suggested that as a national politician, Hays was too busy enjoying his ministerial prerogative of first-class air travel around the country and across the world to do any worthwhile work in Parliament for the folks on the farm he was elected to serve. Newman also wrote in *Maclean's* that Hays was "not really a farmer."

"Hell," Hays later chuckled, "I've always travelled first class. I didn't have to be a federal cabinet minister to do that, and Newman could have found that out if he'd bothered to ask."

As well, Hays was indeed a farmer, and as a farmer, he established several landmarks, the most enduring undoubtedly the development of the Hays Converter, the only purebred beef breed of any consequence to have been developed in Canada and one of only three developed in North America. Hays's Holstein herd, once the largest in Canada at five hundred head, at one time held more world records than any other Canadian dairy herd.

As a livestock exporter, Hays personally opened new markets for Canadian livestock in more than a dozen countries, and he was the first person ever to ship purebred Canadian dairy cattle to Britain, boldly reversing the historic direction of purebred cattle movement; until then Britain's dairy cattle had been considered, by Canadians as well as by Britons, superior to any bred in Canada.

Hays's cattle shipments to Britain reached such proportions that he chartered whole ships to carry them.

While continuing to manage the family dairy farm outside Calgary, Hays expanded his farming operations into Ontario, and his search for new export markets widened. In 1942 he and his brother Tom made the first shipment of Canadian cattle to Mexico. In 1946 they became the first to ship cattle into export markets by air, and a decade later they were North America's biggest exporter of purebred livestock. By then, too, Hays was one of the most successful cattle auctioneers of his time.

As mayor of Calgary, Hays turned the city into virtually the only one of its size in North America with a single municipal government by implementing a widely controversial annexation program. As the first commercial jetliners were introduced, he successfully resisted environmentalists' pressure to move airports from hearing distance of city residential areas by rezoning the area around Calgary's existing airport for commercial development only.

Still, some members of the Opposition and the Parliamentary Press Gallery did have the idea, when he first arrived on Parliament Hill in 1963 from the cowtown of Calgary, that Harry Hays really *was* just a right-wing Alberta bumpkin, an awkward and unsophisticated rustic. And at first glance, the appearance of the short, heavy-set, bespectacled prairie farmer offered no hint that he was anything but an ordinary kind of guy—certainly no obvious policy mover and shaker.

Nor was his grammar always quite correct. He would often use "don't" for "doesn't," for instance; in private, if he thought someone incompetent, he might employ a favourite rude saying: "He don't know shit from paint." Once he said of a bureaucrat in another department: "He couldn't administer a two-hole outdoor shithouse, even if he could call a meeting every time somebody wanted to use it." In his early days in federal politics he sometimes forgot himself, when making speeches, and swore casually (mostly just hells and damns) the way he did at the Rotary Club's more informal luncheons or from the cattle auctioneer's platform with which he was so much more familiar than the cabinet desks in the Commons.

Hays's observers in the Parliamentary Press Gallery were also slow to recognize the fact that he was probably the most widely experienced agriculturalist ever to serve as Canada's minister of agriculture, besides being only the second farmer ever to hold the post up to then. (Alberta farmer Robert Weir held the portfolio in the 1930–35 Conservative government of R. B. Bennett; the third farmer in the portfolio was Albertan H. A. ("Bud") Olson from 1968 to 1972.)

As press gallery pundits would finally realize, Hays was a doer, usually happy, sometimes even exuberant, but always profoundly determined. He could not endure idleness. He once went to Hawaii for a two-week holiday and came back after just three days because he found leisurely lolling on a beach unbearable. Action was his relaxation. As his brother Jack recalled, Hays derived the same enjoyment in going to his foothills ranch as others did in going to their lakeside cabins. "He always said he could get in among a bunch of cattle and they never talked back to him." The same could not be said of his companions in Parliament.

By the time Hays had been named minister of agriculture in 1963, he clearly understood the importance to successful action of careful forethought. That is why, following his own private plan, he said so little in the Commons during his first few months there and accomplished as much as he did once he had the lay of the parliamentary land and the policy needs of farmers figured out according to his own lights.

He also appreciated the role subtle manipulation played in gaining the support of those on whom he depended for getting things done. His sister Virginia remembered, "Harry was a great organizer. He could just get the best out of anyone. I think that's a gift, a gift from God." Some of his less uncritical friends viewed this gift more in the manner of his sister Catherine, as a talent for getting others to do the work of putting his ideas into action. But even those, like his long-time Calgary crony Ed O'Connor, who now and then mentioned Hays's talent for inducing others to do his bidding, did so with appreciative amusement, not resentment. As Hays's special assistant from April 1964 until his resignation in December 1965, following his November election defeat, I had many opportunities to witness his genial gift for drawing the most out of those he worked with.

An important element in Hays's political survival strategy was that image of the barefoot but commonsensical country boy with cheek. Frequently while he held the agriculture portfolio under the cosmopolitan Prime Minister Lester B. Pearson, Hays deliberately and skillfully exploited this image, entirely unfounded in the sophisticated, if rough-hewn, reality of the man. And presenting himself in so disarmingly amusing a light won him some political benefit, especially in western Canada where his political fate lay.

Summing up the goal of his policies for Canadian agriculture, he once said: "We want a flush-toilet, not an outhouse, farm economy for Canada." His words may have shocked sensibilities in the House of Commons, but out in the country where the farmers lived, they were readily appreciated. On another occasion, in a rollicking speech to a Montreal Rotary Club luncheon of top businessmen in the St. James Street financial area, Hays said: "When I first went to Ottawa, they were calling me a right-wing Conservative in a ten-gallon Liberal hat—and a few other things as well. As far as I'm concerned, I'm still the same barefoot boy from the barnyard that I always was."

One who early on had the impression that Hays as minister of agriculture was a gauche bumpkin was journalist-author Walter Stewart, then covering Ottawa for the Toronto *Star Weekly*. Like some other Ottawa journalists, the professionally skeptical Stewart was slow to perceive the real Harry Hays, the restlessly energetic, tirelessly ambitious, skillfully manipulative politician camouflaged behind his façade of barefoot boy from the barnyard.

Stewart was moved to write a cover story in the 4 September 1965 *Star Weekly* about Hays at the height of his activities as agriculture minister. In my role as Hays's special assistant, I arranged for the interviews at both his Calgary home and his five-thousand-acre ranch some fifty miles southwest of the city during Stampede week that July. Describing Hays as he met him for the first time on the lawn of his Calgary home, Stewart wrote: "He is an ordinary-looking man, about five feet, ten inches tall, with 220 pounds of heft and fat laid squarely on a sturdy frame." Joking at his own expense as he often did, Hays said of his penchant for putting on weight: "If I was a Hereford bull, I'd be in great demand."

Stewart noted that Hays was wearing a white sports shirt, grey flannel pants "with a patch on one pocket," short cowboy boots and a Stetson. "His face is round, with open, cheerful features. Behind strong glasses in brown plastic frames his eyes are a clear blue, but the left one is weak and he tends to squint with it, so that he looks as if he were always just about to wink—and that's possible, too. He has a generous mouth, full of regular, white teeth, all his own. They show to advantage when he grins, which is often." I had noticed Stewart studying Hays's unusually even teeth and had sensed he was about to write "store-bought" in his notebook. He laughed and confirmed my suspicion when I pointed out that Hays's teeth were his own.

Stewart pointed out how deceptive any first impression of Hays could be: "At a glance, he is a joyful man, friendly and loud; a shoe salesman, perhaps, or an insurance agent, never a self-made millionaire, a powerful politician, an outstanding administrator." Hays, Stewart found, was "a good talker, a better yarner. . . . He likes to tell reporters who smooth the roughage from his language that they have misquoted him." Stewart also noted that Hays would sometimes rather make a story interesting than strictly accurate and quoted one that Hays frequently told.

> One time we had a three-year drought out here and it was bad, so bad we had three-year-old frogs around here that didn't know how to swim. Well, this time, a friend said, "Come on, Harry, it's time you went to church and prayed for rain." I'm a Catholic, but I hadn't been to church for three years. So I did. I went into the church, and there I was, praying for rain, and pretty soon my friend said, "Hey, you better quit now, Harry, she's starting to cloud up." And so it was. That evening, it began to rain, and it rained for seven days. It got so wet I had to go back to church next Sunday and call it off.

Hays seemed to Stewart

one of the most colorful and contrary characters in a House of Commons full of contrasts. No minister in Ottawa is laughed at more than Hays, and few wield as much power; no minister seems more inept in Parliament, and few get so much done outside it. He is considered the most right-wing member of the Pearson cabinet, yet most of his solutions for Canada's agricultural problems come from left-wing governments in Western Europe. The cattle auctioneer from Pekisko Creek . . . rules a department of 12,000 employees, administers 35 federal acts, distributes $1,000,000 every working day and does it all with crisp authority, although he seems to spend most of his time with his foot in his mouth. He can't answer the simplest question in the House of Commons without evoking gales of laughter, but at a press conference in Winnipeg, he was applauded for his direct and skillful answers.

What manner of man, I wondered, can be bumbling and brilliant, awkward and able, left-wing and right, at the same time?

Stewart's assertion that Hays, in the Commons, frequently put his foot in his mouth was not supported by all other political columnists. As early as July 1964, the thoroughly seasoned political columnist Charles Lynch had written glowingly of a Hays Question Period performance as having "rocked" the Commons with laughter and having left his Opposition critics "limp." Lynch's evaluation of Hays's political skills, written a year earlier than Stewart's, was the opposite of Stewart's. The laughter in the Commons was at his opponent's expense, not Hays's.

The redoubtable Harry, butt of many a Commons joke and jingle for his many absences from the House, blew in from the West and proceeded to demonstrate:

—That he had been doing the nations's business while away from Ottawa, with time out for an operation and to brew the syllabub joy juice that is his annual contribution to the Calgary Stampede.

—That his time was better employed outside the House than it would have been inside it.

—That it's a good idea for a cabinet minister to let his parliamentary critics fester from time to time, and then take them all on in a lump. . . . If other cabinet ministers proceed to emulate Mr. Hays and show up in the House on selected occasions instead of every day, the gain in man-hours worked at cabinet level would be enormous. And, if Mr. Hays is an example, the ministers would come in at the peak of their form. . . . and their tormentors might think twice before going for their guns. Mr. Hays could go down in the books as a greater reformer than Stanley Knowles. . . . While Knowles is trying to rewrite the rule books, Harry makes up his own rules as he goes along.

One of Hays's questioners that day was John Diefenbaker, in his new role as Opposition leader. He apologized for not having been able to get to Calgary and partake of the "Beelzebub" served to the hundreds of friends and acquaintances Hays invited to his annual Stampede breakfast. "We missed you," Hays told teetotalling Diefenbaker; "I'm sure you would have enjoyed the drink very much." Diefenbaker joined in the laughter and then said he would have been frightened away from the special Hays concoction, as news reports said Defence Minister Paul Hellyer had looked confused after partaking. New Democrat Leader Tommy Douglas interjected that Hellyer looked confused even before he partook.

The laughter continued as Hays answered Diefenbaker's question about drought conditions in northern Saskatchewan by pointing out that things were driest around Prince Albert, Diefenbaker's home riding. Manitoba Tory Nicholas Mandziuk wanted to know why Hays had sent a gift of three cows to Russia. Hays replied that during a visit to Russia he had noticed that one Canadian cow produced more milk than three Russian cows, and he hoped the gift cows would persuade the Russians to buy more Canadian cows. The Commons cheered. Hays got in a final shot when Ontario Tory R. A. Webb demanded to know when a program of free milk in schools would be implemented. Hays evoked further laughter and applause when he responded that "due to the very buoyant economy of Canada, most children have so much milk before they get to school that we can't get any more milk in them." As a result, he said, provincial governments, with the final say, were not pressing for a free school milk program.

In time both the Commons and the press gallery developed a new respect for Hays, though he never stopped being a source of good humour. George Bain, parliamentary columnist for the Toronto *Globe and Mail,* wrote that Hays was known around the cabinet room as "Your Friendly Used Cow Dealer." Bain kidded further that Hays had tried to sell an Ayrshire to a visiting Argentinian by telling him that "it had been driven solely by a little old lady with a three-legged stool called Laura Secord." The music played at the Hays used cow lot was "There'll Never Be Anudder You," "I'm in the Moo-o-o-d For Love," "Cold Hands I Loathe (Beside the Shalimar)" and "You've Really Got a Hold on Me."

By the spring of 1965 other Ottawa columnists had discovered some of the country-sly political skills Hays was mastering. The usually skeptical and sometimes irascible Richard Jackson wrote in the Ottawa *Journal:* "Suddenly, after nearly two relatively quiet years in the Commons . . . Hays has begun making speeches which . . . have become 'must' reading on The Hill . . . , all sounding in fond memory nostalgically like something the barefoot boy of far yesteryear used to hear around the cracker barrel in the general store." Jackson reported that those "chuckling most appreciatively" were Hays's fellow politicians—in most cases Conservatives—from his home city of Calgary. "They recall him in his pre-Ottawa days as leading the affluent, almost do-as-you-please pleasant kind of life as North America's leading and most financially successful auctioneer of purebred cattle."

Another Parliamentary Press Gallery columnist, Maurice Western, opened a column in the Calgary *Albertan* as follows:

> It was said of the late Will Rogers that he was a great actor because he never acted. One might say the same of Mr. Harry Hays, the minister of agriculture who orbits irregularly through Ottawa, reducing his colleagues to panic and the Opposition to utter distraction. Mr. Hays [has] long since shattered most of the accepted rules of politics. . . .
>
> The impact of Mr. Hays upon the national capital [is] approximately equal to the impact of the national capital upon Mr. Hays. To Ottawa Mr. Hays is a phenomenon defying explanation: to Mr. Hays Ottawa is "a very strange land."

Western concluded with this summation of the effectiveness of Hays's approach to political debate: "It is scarcely too much to say that Mr. Hays has Ottawa buffaloed. There is some suspicion among frustrated critics that this may well have been his shrewd intention from the beginning." Having written many of Hays's remarks that stretched, when they did not strain or outrage, the conventional parameters of politics, I can attest that, as columnist Western suspected, Hays's intentions were always shrewd.

Stewart suggested that Hays was exploiting prejudice against Parliament to hold his seat there and was "deliberately giving foolish answers in the Commons to maintain his image as an honest country boy caught in the toils of Ottawa slickers." Without agreeing, Hays replied: "Part of the reason I must talk this way is that the Conservatives have done so much to convince the people of the west we have no interest in them, and that's not so."

At the end of his interviews with Hays, Stewart remained fascinated but puzzled.

> There are, it seemed to me, two Harry Hayses. One is a shrewd bargainer, a gifted administrator, an adept politician in the highest sense of that abused word—the sense of a man who works through other people, for other people, and gets things done. The other is a folksy rancher, fresh into town and determined not to be slickered by those crooked city folks, a political ignoramus who resents Parliament because he doesn't understand it and can't control it, a schoolboy who still does poorly in class. . . . Which of these two is the real Harry Hays I don't know, but together they raise a fine ruckus in Canadian agriculture.

In time even Peter Newman had to revise his early assessment of Hays, though he still misreported Hays's character. In the Toronto *Star,* Newman wrote: "Harry Hays has replaced his former arrogance with an earthy humor that has made him popular even among his many political enemies." Hays had at least an average array of human foibles, but arrogant he was not.

Stewart, in his *Star Weekly* cover story, let it be known that despite his doubts and skepticism, he had been impressed by the real Harry Hays. "I came west to spend several days watching Hays at home, and left convinced that this cheerful, contradictory man may yet prove to be the most influential agriculture minister Canada has ever known."

Assuming that Stewart judged Hays with some accuracy, there remains the challenge to discover how an Alberta farm boy from such modest beginnings and with minimal formal education managed to travel so far from where he started out. It can hardly be disputed that Canadian politics was made livelier with Harry Hays one of its practitioners. But there are as well some profound and lasting results, and it is no exaggeration to say that for most farmers in Canada, and for many in the United States, Britain, France, Latin America and elsewhere, agriculture has not been the same since Harry Hays walked barefoot but bold on Parliament Hill.

CHAPTER TWO

FAMILY
ON A
FARM

Some business ventures in which Harry Hays was involved ran into hard times now and again during his early years, leaving him land-poor or credit-poor or cash-poor. But even at the worst of times, during the Great Depression, Hays was never really hard-up, down-and-out, broke-and-hungry poor.

His American-born father, Thomas E. Hays, after a fling at teaching, graduated in medicine from the University of Missouri in 1903. He interned and worked as a doctor in a Kansas City hospital until September 1905; eyesight problems and his love of cattle then overtook his dedication to medicine. One of his brothers, Dan, had recently returned from a visit to Alberta—which in 1905 became a province in the expanding Confederation—enthusiastic about the pioneer region's future prospects. That autumn the two brothers moved north and took up residence in the Carstairs area, approximately twenty miles north of Calgary. Two years later, their father and mother, brothers Claude and Wilton, and pipe-smoking Great-grandmother Hays travelled from Missouri in a settlers' railway car to join Tom and Dan. Their effects included one good all-purpose horse.

The family settled permanently in the community, an area of rolling prairie fields that stretch eastward into an infinity of distance and westward into rounded foothills and pinnacled mountains. Because they did not have enough money to begin farming right away, Dr. Hays sold real estate until he could save enough to start his own dairy operation. Other family members joined Thomas and Dan in the real estate business and soon branched into insurance, grain farming and livestock breeding. During the depression Dan lost a fortune in real estate.

Dr. Hays started his dairy venture on a rented farm near Carstairs. While there he married Sarah Ambriss Foster, a fourth-generation Canadian from Guelph who was teaching in the town. (Sarah's family originally settled on the land now occupied by the Ontario Agricultural College in Guelph.) Their first child, Catherine, was born before Dr. Hays bought his own farm, a mile west and four miles south of Carstairs. On Christmas Day, 1909, Harry Hays was born on the new farm. So, in rapid succession, were his brothers Tom and Jack and sisters Laura, Virginia, Jean and Audrey. All eight Hays children were born in a space of less than ten years.

For the times, the Hays dairy farm was large—an entire section of land, 640 acres—and prosperous. The family home, a large log house already on the land, was later covered with clapboard. There were two dining rooms, each served by the same kitchen. The Hays children ate with their parents in the smaller dining room. Their meals were prepared by their mother, with plenty of help from her daughters.

Before the introduction of electrically run milking machines, the Hayses always had sixteen to eighteen hired hands working on the farm. They were fed in the larger dining room, on the other side of the kitchen. Their meals were cooked by a maid, usually a young farm girl from the community. The maid had a small room of her own in the house, but the hired hands lived in a large bunkhouse containing several separate rooms. Except for their dining room, the Hays house was out of bounds to them.

The farmyard was situated around a coulee with a stream running through it. The main dairy barn was built on the coulee slope on three levels: the farm hands could drive into the upper level with a load of hay, pitch it off into the middle level and then feed it to the cows on the lower level. Nearby there were smaller barns housing horses and pigs. With the development of electric milking machines, the Hayses installed a "Delco plant," a generator powered by an internal combustion engine.

Jack Hays remembered working very hard on his father's farms. "When we were kids, we used to have to work before we went to school and after we got back from school. My father was a great believer that you had to learn how to work to be successful, and he sure worked us." When herding cattle, when Harry was five or six years old, he and his first best friend, neighbour Jimmy Boyle, used to ride double on a horse. Laura said, "They used to dream of when their legs would be long enough to put their feet in the stirrups instead of in the straps." Hays's oldest sister, Catherine, recalled: "Harry could make everybody else work, but he didn't like to do the work himself. I suppose that's why he was so successful. A guy that does his own work never gets anywhere."

Dr. Hays established a dairy in Calgary through which to distribute the milk produced by his Carstairs herd, which, numbering about 140 head, was large for those days. The milk was shipped from the farm in eight-gallon metal cans loaded into a wagon drawn by a team of four horses. In Carstairs the cans were put on a train for Calgary and the Hays Dairy, located on the north side of the Bow River slightly west of today's downtown section.

At the dairy the milk was tested for butterfat content and was paid for accordingly. Catherine recalled that at one point Dr. Hays became concerned about a remarkable reduction in the butterfat content of his milk indicated by the dairy tests, so he put a spy aboard the Carstairs-to-Calgary train. During the trip, he discovered, the trainmen were skimming cream off the top of the milk cans.

It took Harry Hays's father several years to build up his dairy operation. He started the basic Holstein herd with grade animals, that

is, not purebred ones, though they were among the best grade
cows in the country. But in 1911 Dr. Hays took a step that some of
his fellow dairymen considered radical, if not downright foolish. He
bought an expensive purebred Holstein bull in Wisconsin, another
one in the spring of 1914, and more after that. The general feeling
among other dairymen was that the prices for these bulls were
away out of line simply for the breeding of grade-quality cows.

However, Dr. Hays found that the daughters of cows bred by
these expensive purebred bulls weighed 300 to 500 pounds more at
maturity than their mothers. As well, the daughters of these bulls
produced from 2000 to 6000 pounds more milk in a year than their
mothers.

Harry Hays's early observations of his father's genetic ex-
periments with his Holstein herd left a lasting impression on him.
One of his early dreams, in fact, was to work as an animal geneti-
cist on a federal government experimental farm. Catherine remembered Harry as a very young boy talking about what he was going
to do to improve cattle breeding. "He would talk about doing what
nature couldn't do. He could help nature along. You never thought
about it at the time, but afterward you remembered that he'd had
those ambitions all along." She had similar memories about Harry's
childhood interest in politics: "It was his ambition to get into politics
of some kind all his life."

Harry and the rest of the family came by their political awareness
honestly. Both their parents participated in local political activities—Dr. Hays as a stern and lifelong Conservative and Sarah as
a Liberal, equally unyielding about her right to support any candidate, even before women were given the vote in 1918. On election days Sarah, a volunteer worker for her party organization,
would use her horse and buggy to drive Liberal voters to the polls,
and her husband, for the Tory organization, would drive Conservative voters in *his* buggy. Dr. Hays was active in local politics and
for a period served on the Carstairs school board.

Brother Jack recalled that by the time Hays finished grade eight,
he had barely learned to write. His sister Virginia thought his early
school problem was because he had so many other interests, even
then, that he felt being in school was a waste of time. She probably
came as close as anyone to explaining how an Alberta farm boy
managed to accomplish as much as Harry Hays did in only one life-

time when she said that soon after leaving school, he became a self-teaching scholar and remained one for the rest of his life.

Virginia echoed what many people in one way or another expressed about Hays: "Harry always had an open mind. He was able to learn a great deal from people and use that knowledge." That quality of tireless curiosity in Hays was remembered in the condolences of both Prime Minister Pierre Trudeau and Opposition Leader Joe Clark after Hays's death on 4 May 1982. "There was so much scope to Harry and his work," Trudeau wrote to Muriel and their only child, Daniel, "whether it was ranching or Calgary or the government or the Senate or the Liberal party. One just never thought about a time when he would not be putting his mind and his wonderful sense of humour to another project." Clark said of Hays: "He was a strong and innovative man who got things started and saw them through."

The political hot water Hays fell into with women's groups and others across the country in 1980, while he was co-chairman of the joint parliamentary committee on the Constitution, further substantiated a recollection of Jack's from those far-off country-school days: "He was a little bit in trouble all the time. Mischief. He was always that way, and I guess right up till he died, he never lost that." He blamed Hays's poor school record on his frequent expulsion, by one of their country-school woman teachers, for mischievous antics. "I've never forgotten the first time," Hays himself said. "My teacher hung her bloomers on the line, so Hallowe'en night I stuffed them full of rocks, and she put me out."

Catherine agreed that Harry was mischievous to the day he died. "He could tell you the wildest things with a straight face until he'd get you in trouble for believing him." Or, as Hays put it himself, "Generally I've been in trouble all my life."

With a couple of exceptions, the Hays children, with the other rural children, attended school in Carstairs. One of the exceptions happened when Harry was five, in 1915, the second year of the First World War. That school year, his parents sent him and his sister Laura to a Roman Catholic convent boarding school in Red Deer, sixty miles north. Harry never forgot how homesick he was that year—so homesick his parents did not send him back.

The school in Carstairs was a two-storey brick building with four classrooms. The principal was a man and there were four teachers, usually women. In the schoolyard stood a barn where the country kids could leave the horses they either rode to school or, more commonly, as in the Hayses' case, drove, using buggies or wagons in fall and spring and sleighs in winter.

"We had the reputation of being the wildest drivers in the district," Catherine said. "The country kids were always racing. Harry drove, and we hardly ever lost a race. We turned over a couple of times. Once coming out of the school grounds heading home, our buggy locked axles with a coal wagon coming the other way. The buggy shafts broke and the horse kept on going and we all went flying." She broke her arm and had it set in a Carstairs doctor's office a short time later without benefit of anaesthetic.

Once, when Dr. Hays was on the school board, the mayor and an assembly of leading townspeople called upon him with a special plea to stop Harry and the rest of the Hays children from racing other farm children to school in their horses and buggies, out of fear for the safety of all involved.

In winter the Hays children travelled to school in an enclosed van on sleigh-runners, similar to the vehicles milkmen and Chinese laundrymen drove on their delivery rounds. Remembering the five-mile drives in that van, Hays used to joke that he was one of the first school bus drivers in western Canada. The van was entered through a door at the rear, and the Hays children, and often neighbouring children picked up along the way, sat on benches along either side. The van was heated for the long ride with foot-warmers—covered metal trays with hot charcoal brickets inside; they would still be warm for the after-school trip home. There was an isinglass-type windshield at the front and a slot through which to slip the reins.

"We had an old horse that would take us right to school if you didn't touch the reins," Jack recalled—it was the all-purpose horse brought up from Missouri. "Sometimes it would frost up in there. You couldn't see. When the horse stopped we knew we were at school, and we'd just get out the back end."

Every now and again Harry drove too close to the ditch and upset. Then sister Laura angrily refused to ride inside and sat instead on the running board on the back. Then, Catherine said, "Harry would deliberately go over every bump he could find and around the corners as fast as he could to try and throw her off." They had relatives all the way between home and town, and Mrs. Hays would phone them for progress reports. "Well, they've gone by here," she would be told, "but Laura's sitting on the running board."

Harry and Laura fought often, Jack declared, and it seems their arguments never stopped. Laura said they argued about "how a crow would land on a post. Or which post he was going to land on. It was ever thus." At the time of Hays's death, the two had not spoken to each other for three years because of Laura's opposition to Harry's continuing loyalty to Prime Minister Trudeau.

She did not, though, remember her brother too unfondly. "Harry did what he wanted from day one. There was a terrible blizzard in May 1919 in Carstairs. We had five miles to go home, so my father phoned my grandparents, who lived about three-quarters of a mile from town. They were to take us in so we wouldn't chance going home. Sometimes Harry rode a horse because he couldn't get along with us in the buggy. He was riding horseback that day, and he was to come in to our grandparents', too. He wouldn't. But he got home quite safely. He did exactly what he wanted."

CHAPTER THREE

RIDING THE UPPER DECK

The Hays family moved in the summer of 1924 to a new farm, this one also a section—640 acres—and much closer to the dairy market, which would substantially cut back the three hundred dollars a month it was then costing to ship the milk from Carstairs. The new farm was located a few miles south of Calgary's southern outskirts, within sight of the city's taller buildings, at what was known as Turner Siding, near the CPR's Glenmore Station flag stop. Catherine remembered how they could stop the northbound passenger train from Lethbridge by putting up the red flag and ride into Calgary for a fare of twenty-five cents.

Not long after the Hayses had settled into their new home, Harry and Tom learned that a two-day boxing tournament was held every March at the Stampede grounds in Calgary. At about the same time, Hays read in a magazine about a correspondence course in boxing that had been developed by heavyweight champion Jack Dempsey's trainer, Jimmy Deforest. The course cost sixty dollars, a lot of money for fourteen-year-old Hays. But he had made up his mind that he was going to learn to be a boxing trainer by correspondence. He somehow got the money together and sent for the course.

He recruited brothers Tom and Jack to help in his new enterprise, along with a youth named Stu Millington, who lived with the Hayses while his father worked for them, and a young jockey, Charlie Scott. Virginia told of how, when Hays became a boxing trainer, he gathered these boys together and told them that he would have a fitness course, and that he would train them himself. "We had a big living room, and first he decided that's where he'd have the boxing. My mother thought maybe it was a good idea— until the first night. And that was the end of it. So they landed down in the dairy barn. He fixed a ring in the loft and put ropes around it."

Hays proved to be a diligent trainer. Jack weighed 135 pounds when Hays was trying to get him into the 126-pound class. "They used to take me and run me around the farm. They'd drive in the car, and it was a section—four miles around. But they never got me down to that weight, so I had to go into the 136-pound class."

Harry and his boxing team entered the fight tournament at the Stampede grounds. Virginia said: "Tom and Harry were the trainers—they had the towels—and Stu was in the ring. And Stu says, 'Well, now, if the fella starts hitting too hard, what do you do?' Well they said, 'If you think you're getting too much punishment, just fall down. That's what you do. And we'll throw the towel in.' "

Jack remembered Stu's fight:

Stu says to Tom, "Now when I say throw in the towel, you throw it in." So this fella is pretty good on his feet and he boxed pretty good. Stu, he kept running all the time, but he was putting jabs in, and this guy, he let go one awful swing right over Stu's head and Stu hit the floor. He says, "Throw the towel in," and Tom says, "He hasn't even hit ya; get up."

Laura remembered the end of the story. "Stu had to get up and fight. Well, he ended up with two black eyes. Oh, God, he was mad. We were all mad." Virginia, too, still remembered the event:

> I can remember us five girls crying and everything. And Harry'd say, "You're not supposed to be crying, you're supposed to be clapping." We were afraid somebody was going to get hurt. But he did things like that, Harry did. He was always interested in promoting something. Harry had that for two or three years, you know. And he was quite a success at it.

In grade seven or eight at the new Glenmore school, Hays wrote a composition of which he was very proud. Laura recalled: "He said that the day would come when there would be airplanes going across the country and where you could sleep on them, and that they would go around the world. The teacher read it out. This, I think, probably had a great effect on his life because all these smart kids, they just put their heads down and snickered the whole way through. . . . Compare the future achievements of Harry with those of the extremely clever kids that went to school with him."

Nonetheless, Hays continued to have problems at school. Jack remembered Hays's early school disasters.

> When Harry went to school, he got kicked out about once a week. And every time, he'd say to the teacher, "When do I come back?" And she'd say, "Tomorrow morning." But that school teacher used to have trouble with her car. She was a great friend of my mother, and she'd phone up and say, "I can't get my car started. Will you send Harry down to help?" So Harry'd go down and help her. She thought the world of Harry. But she never could handle him. She'd keep expelling him, and he'd always come back the next day.
>
> Harry had to learn to write after he got out of school. He learned how to write and a lot of things after he got out of there. I don't think he'd ever have learned in school.

Laura and Harry were in the same grade, she always at the head of the class and he always at the bottom. She believed Harry had such a difficult time in school because "he couldn't put it on paper."

One day he was to write an exam, and he just couldn't. I used to nearly die. I'd look over and there wouldn't be a damn thing on his paper.

One day something got under the teacher's skin. She had us put all our books away, and she said, "You know, I think there are some of you folks who think you know more than I do. And if there is anybody that does, just stand up." And Harry stood up. So she said, "Get out and stay out." Now this was in June, just before the final exams. So Harry went home. He said, "I can't go back to school." I think he was tickled to death. Miss Martin came up that night and talked to my mother and father. She said, "I just can't have him back unless he apologizes." But Harry wouldn't apologize.

Dr. Hays finally solved this problem by arranging for Harry to simply sit in the classrooms at St. Mary's boys' school in Calgary for the next couple of years and monitor the courses without writing exams. So ended Harry Hays's formal education, except for some short business courses he later took at the Garbutt's Business College in Calgary.

According to Virginia, Hays often regretted that he had not received more formal education. "He was a great reader. When you speak of education, I think in those days there were a lot of self-educated people. He became self-educated. There weren't too many who went to university. Formal education in those days wasn't that important."

Jack related how if anything ever happened at the Glenmore school, "we were always blamed for it, whether we did it or we didn't do it." But this changed the first summer that the Hays boys went on the livestock show circuit. They took to the rails at the end of June, and about the middle of July, the school trustees complained to Dr. Hays. "Some kids had broken into the school and upset the desks and threw ink all over," Jack said. "They came over to my father and he says, 'I don't think it's them. They've been away since June.' Never had any more trouble after that."

□   □   □

Harry Hays was only fourteen when the family moved to the new farm, yet already he had gained some experience in showing cattle. When he was just nine, he had exhibited his animals competitively in the local Carstairs fair. At fourteen he took some show animals to compete in a fair in Red Deer, and the next year, 1925, he showed cattle at the Calgary Exhibition for the first time.

After two summers of working on the new dairy farm so much handier to Calgary and its city-style living, Hays decided that he and his brothers should try their luck with a small herd of show livestock on the summer exhibition trail—much to his father's consternation and angry opposition. He thought they were too young and inexperienced, he doubted the value of their enterprise, and he wanted them to stay home and work for him. Dr. Hays physically tried to prevent Harry and his two younger brothers from loading their livestock onto the railway car the first time they set out on the exhibition circuit in the summer of 1926.

Jack supposed one of his brother's main motivations was his dislike of the back-breaking labour involved in operating the dairy farm—that and how hard their father had always expected his children to work. "I guess that's why Harry got thinking, well, we better make it a little easier in some way." So in open defiance of their father, and almost through the use of physical force to load their animals onto the railway car, Harry, Tom and Jack escaped to the headier life on the livestock exhibition trail.

Laura disagreed with Jack's reference to how hard their father worked his sons.

> That is for dispute. I think they thought cattle showing was adventurous, and it was. They knew absolutely nothing about it. They didn't know what to wash the cattle with, hot or cold water. The first time, they washed the cattle with hot water, which just made their hides like boards. So they used to send Jack around to watch the other guys. Then he'd run back and tell them what they were doing. And that's how they learned.

Many years later Hays told an interviewer what initially inspired him to hit the exhibition circuit. "I was going to school," he said, "and my job for the summer was going to be cleaning out a sheep shed where there were about three thousand loads of manure. It seemed to me there was a better way of earning money."

The previous summer he and Tom took a break from pitching manure and visited the livestock exhibition at the Calgary Stampede. There they saw a professional cattle showman in action for the first time. His name was Art Hay. "He was out that year with the Elgie herd, and we decided then and there that some day we wanted to lick Art. And so I showed cattle. From that time on we continued showing them. At one time we had three show herds travelling in North America. Not only Holsteins. We've also showed Shorthorns; we showed Herefords. We've shown hogs, and we've shown sheep."

But success did not come easily. They took a few animals to the exhibition at the Stampede the next year. Hays said, "We took the worst licking anyone could take. We never got a first"—not then nor for a while to come.

All the same, the next year they set out on the A circuit, where the best herds competed. By then Catherine was working in a florist's shop for ten dollars a week. Harry borrowed twenty dollars from her to get started, but by the time they had done Calgary and Edmonton, they had taken such a trimming that they had to drop back into the B circuit, where the competition was less formidable, to try to recoup. As Catherine remembered, the Hays boys' herd did better at the smaller Red Deer exhibition. "They won some prizes there and got on to the next show."

There was a substantial element of risk in this first major venture into agribusiness. What convinced Hays to try winning prize money with a show herd of cattle was a government program that provided the rail fare home from a livestock exhibition for any farmer and his herd. All Hays had to do was get to an exhibition with his herd. Then, even if he did not win any prize money, he was at least assured of the price of passage home for himself and his cattle. The next year, he and his brothers set out on the A circuit again, and this time they won enough prizes to stay with it.

About that time Art Hay moved west to Alberta to run a CPR farm near Strathmore, and he took the Hays brothers under his tutelage in the art of cattle showmanship. Their acquaintance began at the Calgary Exhibition and Stampede but soon extended across the country. In 1928 and 1929 Art Hay took the Hays brothers with him on the circuit, which included Toronto's Royal Winter Fair, to help them get the experience to travel it on their own. Many years later Hay recalled:

I think I knew Harry and Tom better than anybody, including their own parents. Jack was the cow man. He couldn't sell peanuts in the monkey section of a zoo. But he did the work. Tom could sell anything. Harry did the talking. It always burned me up when people said, "Well, Harry made his money out of real estate." Harry during those early days didn't have one cent to rub against another. But Harry was the man that put Holsteins in business in world markets. He had more gall than a canal horse. He was a genius. A Bank of Montreal fellow once said Harry knew more about financing than any bank manager in Canada. He could finance on nothing and make you feel happy. Once some Mexicans were so disappointed they were ready to shoot him, but he wound up selling them another five hundred head.

In 1931 Hays—then only twenty-one—and his two younger brothers travelled seventeen thousand miles with two herds on the move, one on the A circuit and the other on the B. Among the prizes they won were one All American and one Reserve. In 1932 they showed against fifty-four other herds at the Canadian National Exhibition in Toronto and won a hatful of red ribbons. By 1933 Jack was responsible for all the feeding and fitting of the travelling animals. Hays used to say of Jack, then seventeen, that he knew his business so well, he could bring a herd home after fifteen thousand miles of travel in better condition than when they started out. By then, too, Tom was taking a small tent and the necessary utensils to cook for other showmen wherever they went, and that helped to pay expenses. Art Hay remembered how homesick Tom used to get in the early years of travelling. "He would be sitting in the tack room crying and calling his mother on the phone to come and get him."

Hays and his brothers travelled the livestock show circuit every summer until the war broke out, and then they continued showing after it. They travelled from June through until the Royal Winter Fair in Toronto in the autumn. "We'd travel sometimes twenty thousand miles," Jack remembered. "We'd travel from coast to coast in Canada, down in the States, all over." They exhibited against competitors—who often had much more wealth behind their show herds—in cities as widely separated as Saskatoon and Waterloo, Iowa, and Victoria and Springfield, Massachusetts. The prize money they won always went to pay their way. Fortunately they won lots of prizes. But they still had to make sacrifices to stay on the road.

"We all worked for nothing," said Jack. "Sometimes we didn't get three square meals a day." They travelled by freight train, living in a cattle car while on the move. "We used to fix a car up—put ticks [straw-filled mattresses] in it. We'd start out in our car and we ended up in it. We slept above the animals on the deck. My wife says now I never want to eat out on a picnic because we ate with the bugs long enough. Harry was like that, too."

Laura said that her brothers got up to their usual tricks while on the exhibition circuit. "On the midway there was all kinds of sham things. So the boys put up a sign saying, 'Come and see the hairless dog.' You had to climb up on three bales of straw to look. And there was a hotdog. They'd charge a nickel to see it. A nickel was a lot of money. A hotdog was ten cents."

The contract with the railway for hauling the show herd between exhibitions put a limit on the number of persons allowed to ride in each cattle car. Jack remembered problems developing from this arrangement.

> You were only supposed to ride one on a car, and there was always three or four of us. We had hay up in the back, and we'd put a hole in there and crawl in at the back. But we got caught in Medicine Hat once.
>
> Harry was there. He says, "I never seen those guys before." And the policeman took us up to the station. We went back into the restaurant, washed our hands and out the back door. Before the policeman woke up, we were on our way.

Travelling the exhibition circuit with a prize-winning herd gradually built up the Hays name in agricultural circles, as exhausting as the travelling might be. It also gradually "produced a lot of dough," as Jack remembered.

"We broke records, too. You milked the cows travelling. They were looked after just like they would be in the barn. They were really looked after better. They'd be bedded down. We carried water. We used to feed these cattle three times a day. We used to blanket them." Some of the animals that were taken on the circuit yearly seemed to know when it was time to head off on a new trip. "You'd just put the halter rope over their neck," Jack said, "and they'd walk into the freight car. They were broke real good."

Agriculturalist, politician, author and former lieutenant governor of Alberta Grant MacEwan, who succeeded Hays as mayor of Calgary, remembered first encountering him on the exhibition circuit. "I was completing my university work and taking the family herd on the fair circuit. We had different breeds of cattle, but we were attending the same shows."

Hays was winning more, by a good deal.

Hays cattle were at the top at that time. Then immediately after that I was with the University of Saskatchewan and doing a lot of judging. I would frequently meet Harry and his cattle at the shows. I would be the judge.

I remember accusing him once of stealing a bale of hay from me. I reminded him of that in later years, and he said, "Oh yes, I remember that."

He was an outstanding showman. Nobody could fit an animal for a show better than Harry Hays. Nobody could present it before the judge better. He was an expert in setting an animal up so the animal would look its best.

CHAPTER FOUR

EXPANSION OVERSEAS

One of Harry Hays's least-publicized but most enduring successes was his forty-eight-year marriage to Muriel. Anyone who observed them together over any length of time could not escape noticing their deep enjoyment of each other.

Calgary *Herald* columnist Merv Anderson first met Muriel in 1959, when as a city hall reporter he went to the Hayses' home for Harry's announcement that he was running for mayor. "I can say I liked Harry, respected him," Anderson said, "but I can almost say I loved Muriel. Harry looked more plain-folks than Muriel, but he was tougher to get to know."

Arthur Smith, then the Progressive Conservative member for Calgary South, agreed to manage Hays's mayoralty campaign, and he went to the Hays home every morning for breakfast meetings.

(When they sold the dairy farm in 1957, the Hayses kept seventeen acres and continued to live in the rambling old two-storey farm house they had taken over from his parents.) Muriel would cook bacon and eggs, and she would often order Harry not to start talking about campaign business until Smith could finish eating. "I doubt if anyone knows what a strength Muriel was," Smith recalled. "She'd sit quietly and listen, and if he got raspy, she'd take him aside and speak to him and calm him down."

A petite and vivacious woman with dark hair and sparkling brown eyes, she provided Hays with a stable emotional home base that other men might envy. Although strong-willed in her own right, she was even-tempered and had a sense of humour to match his. He shared everything he did with her, and she supported him in everything, though often not before questioning him adroitly to be clear where she might fit into his scheme of things.

On the Macleod Trail not far from the Hays dairy farm was the Glenmore Community Hall, where what Muriel Bigland remembered as "real old country dances" were held regularly, attracting all the young people in the community. One night when he was about eighteen, Harry found time to attend and met Muriel, a year his junior and the daughter of a CPR locomotive engineer. Neither was struck blind by the other. Although it was several years in blooming, this meeting was the beginning of a lifelong romance.

"I knew his sisters. When you're in a group of people, you don't just see someone and swoon. I knew him for quite a while before I really went out with him. There was just a group of us. We went to dances, to the moving picture show, to eat, that sort of thing." Even that early in their relationship, Hays's work in agriculture often kept them apart. "He'd leave whenever the shows started, so I didn't see him all summer."

Auctioneer Archie Boyce, later a partner with Hays for a few years, remembered one of Muriel's early impressions of Hays's family. "That whole Hays family—a great bunch to kibbitz. Muriel said when she first went there—they invited her to dinner—they'd reach right over in front of her to grab something."

Hays's son, Dan, their only child, remembered how uproarious some of the family dinners could be. He hinted that he thought it might have influenced his father's behaviour towards him.

He was always careful not to let our relationship become bad, where we fought and disagreed and walked away. He would back off. But his relationship with his brothers and sisters sometimes was pretty tense.

They really did fight like hell. They would all have supper together on Sunday, and they would really get into some very serious quarrels, it seemed to me at the time. I was four, five, six years old, but I remember to this day. They yelled and they were unreasonable with each other. But they seemed to get along well in the final analysis.

Muriel and Harry decided to get married in 1934, about six or seven years after their first meeting. (After Hays had become mayor of Calgary, a reporter asked Muriel when he had proposed to her. Her reply: "I can't remember.") One reason for the timing was the initial cattle-selling trip to Britain that Hays had planned for that time. "He thought he might stay over there and wondered if I would come over and join him, if he did," Muriel said. "So we thought we'd get married."

In the end they were wedded twice. The first marriage took place on the CPR farm operated by Hays's cattle showman friend, Art Hay, near Strathmore. That was on 28 February 1934. Hays being a Roman Catholic and Muriel an Anglican, they were married by a United Church minister. In his introductory remarks to the Edmonton Liberal convention in January 1965, Hays gave this version of the marriage.

> I'd been going with Muriel for seven years. We couldn't afford to get married. She was working in a furniture company, and I was pitching manure out at the farm. And when I suggested to her that I was taking three carloads of cattle to Montreal and then we were going over in the boat, she said, "Well, what if it's a flop? How you gonna get back?"
>
> I said I could work my way back. I could wash decks and do all that sort of thing. And she said, "Well, maybe you can, but maybe we better get married before you go over there." So I picked her up at Neilson's furniture store and we drove out to Strathmore and we got married.

At seven-thirty that evening we did up the dishes. I had a car that I'd purchased in 1929, a Ford, and she drove back to Calgary and I caught the freight at Strathmore. I remember the brakeman that day—I said, "I'm on my honeymoon." So he said, "Well, where's your wife?" And I said, "Well, she's bin to England before." This is a true story. We didn't tell anybody but our friends. Just the two people that stood up for us.

At Montreal Hays learned that he did not need to go over to London, and when he returned to Calgary, the couple were married again, this time more formally in a Roman Catholic ceremony at St. Ann's Church, but not in the main auditorium. Because Muriel was Anglican, they were married in the vestry. It was April thirtieth. "And that's when we had our wedding celebration," Muriel remembered.

After their weddings, Muriel remained an Anglican, and Harry a Catholic. Asked which date they celebrated as their anniversary, Muriel laughed, "That was a good thing for Harry. When it was February, he said our anniversary was in April. When April came along, he said it was February. He didn't have to worry about it. He had another one to fall back on all the time."

For a few months the newlyweds lived in an apartment near downtown Calgary. Then in the fall of 1934 they moved into a small house on the Hays dairy farm that had been converted from a granary. "It had a kitchen and a bedroom and a living room, that's all," Muriel remembered.

She knew little about farming until she married Harry, but in keeping with the times, she had worked for a living since she was seventeen. "I was a comptometer operator. In those days they were the new thing for calculating. We used to go into companies that had trouble with their balances and do all their calculating for them. It was much faster than doing it by hand." As the depression deepened, Muriel gave up this part-time job for a full-time one at the Neilson Furniture Company, where she was working when she and Harry were married. She was an office worker there for about five years while Harry carried on with his various farming activities. Then she traded places with his sister Laura: Muriel did the office work at the dairy farm after Laura married and went to work at Neilson's.

With so many children in the family, life was never dull around the Hays farm. "Harry had a very fine mother," Muriel remembered. "She always had twice as many people there as she had children because they all had friends. Lots of times you'd get up in the morning and go over to her place, and she maybe would have baked eight or nine pies before any of us even got up—the women, anyway. Harry used to get up at 4 A.M. and milk, and his brother Jack did, too."

Although Muriel was a farmer's wife from 1934 onward, she never became involved in farm work beyond keeping the books. She did not cook for farm hands or help with the milking, and she did not even feed the chickens. "We did keep chickens, but they were in the chicken-house and we had a man that looked after them."

It was tough times. You didn't have too much money to spend. You had to work hard to make a living. You didn't take holiday time, you just took the odd day off once in a while.

We were very happy, though. We got enough to eat and we had a good place to sleep and enough clothes to wear. What else did you need when you were young? You always entertained your friends. In those days people didn't go out for entertainment; they entertained one another. We'd go to different places and have parties. We didn't have liquor and things like they have today. We didn't need them.

Even in those early days, Hays spent much of his time travelling. As Muriel put it: "He travelled. Always did travel." He never stopped travelling until his death. Muriel did not accompany him at first because they could not afford it. "And he travelled the exhibition circuits with loads of cattle. He didn't travel any other way. They had to look after the cattle. When you had good cattle, you looked after them yourself. The men could, if they wanted to, go and ride in the caboose. But if you were a good cattleman, you travelled in the boxcars with the cattle. Harry had to do those things.

"But I didn't."

□   □   □

Once Harry Hays had completed the often painful years of his formal education, his appetite for learning was never again fully satisfied. One of the things he most wanted to learn at this beginning stage in his career appears to have been how to make a living without having to work for his father. Muriel remembered that "work was all his father believed in. He didn't believe in fun. He was against that. Harry and his brothers connived a little bit to get out of working on the dairy farm." Dr. Hays could grow seriously angry at any suggestion of a holiday, even a day's outing to nearby Banff.

Nor was it very long before Hays was confronted, along with millions of others, with a new incentive to work mightily for his survival. He was going on twenty when the Wall Street crash of October 1929 formally introduced to Canada and the rest of the world the Great Depression. By 1933 the depression had put the Hays dairy operation into some difficulties, and a major fire that burned their big barn to the ground did not help, though fortunately the dairy cattle were saved and were temporarily housed in Calgary Stampede barns.

Building a new barn, however, turned out to be an almost insurmountable challenge. The insurance on the burned barn did not quite cover the outstanding mortgage; the family already owed money to the bank and could not borrow more. Creditors were getting restless by then. It was decided that, despite whatever differences in his approach to work he might have with his father, Harry, then twenty-three, should take over the management of the farm. "The reason was for the creditors," Laura recalled. "Harry came in with some ideas that weren't very good, but looked good to the creditors, which was taking milk to town by horse and buggy and letting the truck go. We couldn't pay the gas bill. So he took it in by horse, which only lasted about three months. But it satisfied the creditors."

Laura remembered how the rather desperate solution to their broken fortune was arrived at. The Hays family held a meeting. "I remember my two uncles, my mother and father—and I think Harry was there. And I was there to take notes. My mother said, 'Let's just take the cattle and tie them up to fence posts and milk them.' That didn't go over very big. My uncles said, 'Let's sell them all,' and that didn't go over very big." So Dr. Hays was finally driven to borrow from one of Calgary's wealthiest citizens, Senator Patrick Burns.

Laura recalled that Senator Burns had a business manager named Nowers. When her father turned to Burns for help, Nowers would never put through the phone calls. "There was always some excuse because he knew what we wanted. But Patty Burns used to go to eight o'clock mass, and so did my dad." So one Sunday morning Dr. Hays told Burns at church that he wanted to talk to him afterward. Burns invited Dr. Hays to follow him home after mass, and there the request for an $18,000 loan for the new barn was made. "So Patty Burns says, 'You'll have the cheque tomorrow.' And that's how we started up again."

Not long before that, Hays had become Alberta fieldman for the Dominion Holstein-Friesian Association, the beginning of a long relationship with various farm organizations across Canada, and probably one of his inspirations for embarking upon the livestock export business. But he had to give up the fieldman job when he took over management of the family farm.

Many years later he explained why, only the following year, 1934, and just twenty-four years old, he had taken the long gamble of shipping the first dairy cattle ever from Canada for sale in Britain. In an interview for the *Family Herald* in July 1965, he was asked what he felt was the most useful tool he had brought to the job of minister of agriculture from his long career in farming.

I've always had to make a living, and I made it. I didn't have any training in agriculture. When we would bog down producing milk and had to support ourselves by some other means in agriculture, we investigated other activities and we went ahead and attacked them. For instance, back in 1932 I remember taking twelve head of heifers into the stockyards because we didn't think it paid to feed them for the winter. After they were there eight days, the commission firm phoned me and said they couldn't sell them. We had a bill of eighteen dollars for keeping them. I went in on a saddle horse and I drove them home. They were good heifers that would bring three or four hundred dollars today, and I took them down to a bush and I shot them all, then we covered them up with manure and we burned them. This then started our adventure in selling cattle to Great Britain.

The risk of sending good cows to such a far-off market was worth it; Hays far preferred selling cows to shooting them.

His continuous self-education by reading widely had led him to subscribe to the *Scottish Farmer*. It was that magazine's pages that gave him the idea for his first livestock export venture.

At that time the same kind of heifer that could not be sold for any price in Calgary was being sold in Aberdeen for about £30 a head, and at that time the pound was worth $5. We just investigated the shipping costs, and we found people who had cattle to sell. And that's how we started.

It was the same with fox furs. I remember in 1933 that you couldn't sell a fox fur. Nobody in this country could afford to wear the pelt. I discussed this with our largest fox grower, Mr. Colpitts, who had foxes in the Maritimes and in the west, too. We helped merchandise his fox furs in Europe—in London, Paris, Rotterdam, Amsterdam. We peddled them in suitcases. We did this in the winter months, and in the summer months we showed cattle.

Jack Hays recalled that first cattle boat trip to Britain. "It took us twenty-five days. We started out in Edmonton and went to Birken-head, England. We had to sign on the boat at that time as one of the crew, so the captain had control of you. You got paid one shilling. It took eleven days on the water. You had to work whether you were seasick or not."

Harry and Jack had some fourteen hundred head on that trip. At Montreal they met brother Tom on his way back from a not very successful trip abroad peddling fox furs. Tom told Harry that there was no need for him to go to England that trip. Hays was happy enough about that; he had just married, and he went back to Calgary and Muriel.

Hays related his experiences as a neophyte cattle exporter in his 1965 speech to the Edmonton Liberal convention.

I had a wild idea. In 1934 imagine any fella from Calgary, Alberta, a farmer who didn't know much about selling anything, would take a shipload of cattle all the way across to Aberdeen. During the next seven or eight years we shipped a lot of cattle over there, and in July of '39 I'd made $100,000 during the depression, and I was pretty proud of this.

And so was my wife. She quit working in the late fall of '38 and she was pregnant [Dan was born 24 April 1939], and there was just nothing could stop us. A Canadian trade commissioner had suggested that maybe we weren't doing this job quite right—that we should leave these cattle in Cheshire, just outside Birkenhead, and let them freshen up a bit. Then we could sell them to better advantage.

So he suggested that we should leave them there at the home of a German baron. And we did this. In 1939 when war was declared, the baron shot all the cattle, and he flew to Germany. I'd borrowed $60,000 and had everything in the pot. So in 1940 I had a wife, a new baby, no money, and we had a war on our hands. Now that's the kind of a fella you've got as minister of agriculture.

Seasickness almost drove Tom out of the export business when he was barely started. After sailing to Europe with suitcases filled with fox furs, he wrote home saying farewell to all his family and advising them that they would probably never see him in Canada again unless someone built a bridge across the Atlantic. When he did at length return by ship, he was again seasick all the way across.

Hays had other setbacks now and then in his cattle export business. Once, just after he had completed a large sale of cattle to Argentina, the dictator Juan Perón froze all currency exports from his country, and Hays was never able to get the proceeds back to Canada. In January 1952 the Hays brothers put forty-one Holstein calves on a plane bound for the estate of Count Gaetano Marzotto for his Societa Fondiaria Agricola Industriale at Portogruaro in Italy. All were lost when the plane crashed and burned while landing at Pisa. Undaunted, the Hayses gathered together some three hundred Holstein calves and sent them to Italy that May by ship from Montreal.

Quite by quirky chance, for a time during the Chinese-Japanese war of the late 1930s, Hays became a partner in the export business with Harry Veiner, who as mayor of Medicine Hat later won fame for exploits like foot-racing a quarter horse and wrestling an alligator. The two men were having coffee one day in a small restaurant run by a Chinese; in this and similar restaurants all over the prairies, tin can coin banks labelled "China Relief Fund" were kept beside the cash registers. Hays and Veiner wondered what happened to the cash going into those cans. They investigated, and discovered that the fund organizers had more than $1 million on their hands and little idea how to spend it. "So we thought we'd try to sell the Chinese some cattle," Hays said. "We set up a company called Omega Export-Import and did pretty well." On one occasion they sent a whole shipload of cattle to China. The ship had to steal into the Chinese port under cover of darkness because of the war, but managed to unload its cargo safely.

By the end of the Second World War, Harry Hays had become a seasoned international livestock trader. He had made his first shipment of cattle to Mexico in 1942 and had since, with the help of Spanish-speaking employees, extended his sales activities to other Latin-American countries as well as to Europe. He wrote an article for the *Holstein-Friesian Journal* in February 1944 about his first trip to Mexico, which he made by plane, his favourite mode of travel.

I left Chicago at 7:30 in the morning and in eight hours was safe on the ground in Dallas, Texas. I left Dallas at 7:30 next morning and just before arriving in Monterey some five hours later I got my first glimpse of Mexican Holsteins from 2000 feet up. They looked awfully close to the ground.

Mexico is almost a different world. What you see is a city so old, with so much history mixed in with its very dust, that affairs of today seem but brief incidents. You get a new perspective. In and around Mexico City I saw no less than ten stables, or ranches as they are called, milking anywhere from 300 to 1000 head. It is quite a sight to see fifty barefoot milkers sit down at once to extract milk from 700 cows.

On some of his trips to Mexico, Hays would occasionally take time out to spend a day at the horse races. "You don't even have to visit the mutuels to bet," he recalled. "A waiter comes along, serves you with what you want and then makes your bets for you, always returning with the tickets, of course." Tom reported that the track in Mexico City was in some ways even more attractive than the one at California's Santa Anita.

During this time Hays began to appreciate the importance to his cattle export business of being closer to the centre of the market than Calgary was. From 1945 he began spending more and more time in the Toronto area, though still operating the Calgary dairy farm with the help of good farm workers. He eventually owned five farms near Toronto. He persuaded Jack to move to one of them near Brampton and lured Tom from the operation of an Edmonton nightclub to join him and Jack in an expanded export business, Hays International Ltd.

Although Muriel and son Dan visited him there several times, she resisted moving to Ontario until Harry was settled somewhere permanent; "I wasn't going to live in a trailer." She and Dan eventually took the train from Calgary to Oakville to stay at the end of 1946, spending New Year's Eve on the train and arriving at Oakville on New Year's Day. By then Harry had been working the Ontario end of his business for nearly two years.

In the spring of 1946 a young veteran of the U.S. Army Air Forces from Philadelphia, Terry Goodwin, approached Harry and Tom in the lobby of the Royal York Hotel, where Hays always stayed when in Toronto. Goodwin knew about their cattle export business. He told them he was planning to buy a war surplus DC-3 twin-engined cargo aircraft and asked whether they would be interested in hiring him to fly some of their cattle abroad. The Hays brothers decided, why not.

A few weeks later they loaded six Holstein bulls onto the plane at Toronto's Malton Airport. The work of getting the animals into the plane was surrounded with an air of excitement. One of those caught up in that spirit was Hays's son, Dan, then seven years old. The door of the plane was finally closed, and the craft taxied to the end of the runway. But instead of taking off, it taxied back to the Hays party who stood waiting to watch the takeoff. Dan had been discovered hiding on the plane. He was disembarked, and Goodwin flew the cargo of bulls to Havana for delivery to Cuba's Department of Agriculture. As far as the Hays brothers were aware, that was the first time anyone had ever shipped cattle by air anywhere in the world, and it was only the first of dozens more air shipments to various Latin American and other countries during more than a decade of steadily expanding export sales for their company.

Sometimes the flights could be dangerous. Hays spoke of once flying into Chile in a DC-3 with a bull that weighed 2700 pounds. "The plane couldn't go over the mountains, so we had to go through the mountain passes, and all the way through one of my boys held a pistol to the forehead of the bull in case anything went wrong. Why hell, if the bull got loose, he'd have gone right up to the cabin and tried to fly the plane."

In February 1963 Tom Hays listed these export shipments he had supervised, personally or by long-distance telephone, on a typical business day: two carloads of cattle plus one thoroughbred horse from his Oakville farm by rail to Mexico; nine heifers and one bull by truck from Oakville to Miami and from there by plane to Lima, Peru; and a ship carrying 450 Canadian cattle, valued at more than $200,000, from Saint John, New Brunswick, bound for Cuba. Tom could point out that export sales by Hays International had never fallen below $1 million a year since 1956 and had reached nearly $3 million in each of the previous two years. The company was North America's biggest exporter of purebred livestock, selling Canadian cattle in twenty-three countries. Hays had personally gone on selling expeditions to sixteen of them. Harry and Tom were the first North American exporters of cattle to Scotland, Spain, Italy, Israel, China, Brazil, Peru, Argentina, Uruguay, Colombia, Ecuador and others.

But in 1963 Harry Hays was no longer directly involved in the business. He had relinquished his interests to Tom in 1957, partly because he did not enjoy living in Oakville and, more importantly, because in 1950, unaware of it, he had contracted tuberculosis.

"He worked too hard because he was ambitious," Muriel recalled. "We went through some bad times down there. When you're starting out on anything, it's not easy. He didn't know he had tuberculosis until they examined him." TB was customarily treated in sanitariums, with lots of quiet and rest and little in the way of drugs. Hays felt that if he was going to be confined for a year in a sanitarium, he would rather spend it in the old Baker San across the Bow River from Bowness, in familiar territory. The family was back in Calgary by New Year's Eve, 1950.

Hays's Calgary doctor told him that since his TB was not at the contagious stage, he could take his treatment at home on the farm, provided he got at least fourteen hours of rest every day. Muriel said that Hays showed great fortitude during that year. He did not sleep all he should have, and he did not literally stay right in bed, either, but he was very careful not to overwork himself, and he took his medicine. The illness gradually cleared up, and he had no more trouble with it for as long as he lived.

Previous to his bout with TB, Hays had been a heavy cigarette smoker. He switched to cigars after his illness and gave up smoking altogether after he became a senator at age fifty-six.

CHAPTER FIVE

ALCARTRA AND MAKING MONEY

Harry Hays undertook many money-making schemes during his early adulthood, not so much to make a grand profit as to simply keep body and soul together during the Great Depression. First and foremost, though, he was a farmer, with an endless curiosity about animals and their genetics; this interest finally paid off with a renowned cow named Alcartra Gerben, but not before Hays had turned over other stones.

Hays and his brothers, rumour had it, once thought of bootlegging during Prohibition. Muriel remembered the story. "They were going to take some liquor across the line. They got it over there, in the boxcar with the cattle, but they thought, no, they better not do that, they'd better bring it back. So they did. They got cold feet."

Harry and Tom once contracted to supply ten polar bears to a circus in England. They paid Eskimos in far-northern Canada a thousand dollars to catch the bears but then were unable to obtain a permit to ship them out of Canada. Another deal was to catch wild horses running loose on Indian reserves in the Alberta foothills, break them in and sell them to the Russian army. Once when Hays was holding the haltershanks of two wild horses, they reared away from him. He held on to both, but dislocated his shoulders, one so badly that some decades later he required surgery to correct it. But this time they were able to complete the deal, and they did sell their horses to the Russians.

Tom, after stints in a greenhouse and on a used-car lot, joined Harry as co-owner of an Edmonton nightclub known as The Barn. Both also put money into the Beverly coal mine at the bottom of the North Saskatchewan River valley in Edmonton, but a combination of cave-ins, underground floodings and labour troubles cost them this investment. Harry Hays was once more left dependent on his own farming skills and experience.

With the outbreak of the Second World War in 1939 and the economic upsurge that came with it, Hays, like most others, found his fortunes improving. In 1941 he started a sideline that paid him to continue his self-education. He broadcast a fifteen-minute daily program, "The Fruitful Earth," on Calgary radio station CFAC, over a telephone line from his office on the farm. Weekdays he covered farm topics, but on the Sunday program he turned to philosophy.

Muriel said "he would study like mad on philosophy for the Sunday program." He read Schopenhauer, Voltaire, Will Durant, Plato and Aristotle, among others, often quoting passages over the air. He also occasionally found use for the irreverent poetry of Odgen Nash. (He stated in 1965: "I can quote most of the dirty stuff from Ogden Nash." And that same year, while flying back to Calgary after a political rally, he quoted Nash to me at length from memory.) Hays continued the broadcasts until 1945, when his travelling forced him to give them up.

In 1943 the president of the Alberta Swine Breeders' Association, Bill Hudson, presented a baby pig to Hays, then president of the Canadian Swine Breeders' Association, as a mascot for his radio program. Hays promptly named the piglet Fruity and offered her to the Calgary War Loan Committee to help sell Victory bonds. During the Fall Livestock Show and Fair at the Stampede grounds that

October, Fruity brought in $155,000 in just ten minutes of bond sales.

By now the name of Harry Hays and the reputation of his cattle were widely known in agricultural circles right across Canada and into the United States. Hays had also been a dominant figure in various farm organizations. In 1937 he had been a founding member of the Alberta Poultry Breeders' Association, and in February 1942 he was elected to his fifth term as president. He served several terms as president of the Alberta Holstein Breeders' Association and also spent two years as chairman of the Calgary Board of Trade's agricultural bureau.

Early in the war he was elected president of the Canadian Swine Breeders' Association, and from that position presided over an enormous increase in Canadian pork production for consumption in Britain, to make up for wartime shortages there. It was known as the "Bacon for Britain" campaign. By the spring of 1944 Hays— who was ineligible for military service both because he was a farmer and because of eyesight problems—could point to much evidence of the success of Canada's hog producers in this war-effort task. For only the second time in its existence up to then, the Canadian Swine Breeders held their annual meeting in Calgary. Hays informed the forty delegates that in 1943 Canada had marketed 7,149,120 hogs for a gross revenue of $178,748,000—or a little more than $16 for every man, woman and child in the country; it had been the best year in the association's history.

Hays in his speech made a plea for what had become his dominant agricultural interest: better—that is to say, more commercially practical—genetics in farm animals. Hogs had made many Canadians prosperous, he noted, but it was now the job of purebred hog breeders to ensure that commercial breeders received the necessary quality of breeding stock if Canadian production were to maintain its competitive edge in world markets once the war was over.

At the same time, Hays, then thirty-four, was completing the development of the finest collection of Holstein genetic material in Canada, and perhaps in the world, on his Calgary dairy farm. By 1944 Hays and Company had five cows in the mature class of the Canadian Holstein-Friesian Association's honours list, though the star of the Hays herd would not make her play for world fame until the following year. In Alcartra Gerben, Hays would find testimony to his emphasis on genetics in livestock productivity.

Hays purchased her from a disbanding farm herd at Didsbury, Alberta, at a sale that ended on New Year's Eve, 1944, in twenty-two-below-zero weather. Hays bought all the purebreds the farmer had. One, five-year-old Alcartra Gerben, had just calved.

Hays was driving back to Calgary to keep a date with Muriel for a New Year's Eve party. Then, as Grant MacEwan related, he remembered something. "He said, 'By God, I wonder if they'll know enough to milk that cow out tonight. If she's left unmilked, it's going to hurt her.' So what's he going to do? Continue on to Calgary and keep his date with his wife, or go back and get this cow milked out? . . . He was a very, very unpopular fellow when he got to Calgary and it was too late to go to the party."

"We had a barn that was warm," Jack Hays said. "The cows would sweat in the barn, so we clipped them all over, and when we clipped Alcartra, she was just lousy. The lice—you'd never seen anything like it. We cleaned her all up. Her production went up two weeks after we had her in there. And then she just started to go to work."

Before he bought Alcartra Gerben, Hays was aware that her sire had been a Hays bull, and as her milk production continued to improve, he felt certain he might have a winner on his hands. On 25 March 1944 he launched an all-out challenge of the world record 1402 pounds of butterfat production by a single cow. It was held by an American animal, the Carnation Milk Company's Carnation Ormsby Butter King, and was set in 1936. Challenging the record meant milking Alcartra Gerben for a measured time of 365 days. She had to be milked every six hours—four times a day around the clock for one full year. And how the milk flowed from her!

Jack took responsibility for her milking, but he had some help in Eugene Okumura, who had immigrated from Japan in 1921. The wave of anti-Japanese feeling after Pearl Harbor forced him to leave his Vancouver dry-cleaning business and flee inland to Calgary, where Hays hired him to work on the dairy farm. Okumura was taught how to milk, and he milked Alcartra Gerben through most of her testing trial. He worked the rest of his life for the Hays brothers.

During her year-long test, Alcartra's milk production in pounds equalled her own weight approximately every three weeks. Her daily butterfat output produced about four and a half pounds of butter, enough to fill the wartime daily butter rations of nineteen families. From the beginning of the test period through October, Alcartra Gerben's daily milk yield varied less than one pound per milking. Then from November to the end of January, her daily yield gradually declined. During this whole period she had been milked by machine, but now, when it appeared she might fall short of the record, the Hays brothers set Okumura to hand-milking her. Her output immediately recovered.

At five o'clock on Saturday afternoon, 24 March 1945, the final milking took place. The news media, officials of the Alberta agriculture department and others—Tom had taken a break from his Edmonton nightclub; Grant MacEwan was also there—gathered in the big Hays barn. Jack presided on the stool beside Alcartra. Reporters scribbled notes, cameras flashed, and both Calgary radio station CFAC and the CBC's farm commentator, Peter Whittall, broadcast live from the scene as Jack stripped the last drop from the cow.

Over the 365-day test, Alcartra Gerben had produced 27,748 pounds of milk, containing an average 5.07 per cent butterfat—a total of 1409 pounds of it, 7 pounds more than the Carnation cow's world record, and the equivalent of 1761 pounds of butter. Alcartra had done it!

The final test milking was followed by a celebration banquet thrown by the Hayses in the ballroom of Calgary's Palliser Hotel. Five hundred people attended and joined in a toast to Alcartra with her own milk. She was the first Alberta cow and only the third cow in Canada to set a world production record. Her performance and the attendant publicity were well worth the expense of the banquet. Later, one of her calves sold to a buyer from England for $10,000, another sold for $8,000, another for $7,000, and in 1947, when Hays decided to disband the dairy herd and concentrate on the cattle exporting business, Alcartra and one of her sons sold for $20,000 each.

Yet Alcartra Gerben was not the sole winner then in the Hays herd. Doncrest Peg Top Burke had set a world record for butterfat production on twice-a-day milking while with a previous owner. And Hays Snowden Lady 2nd retained the Canadian record for percentage of butterfat content, with 5.21 per cent; in this category, Alcartra Gerben was only second in the country. Of the some three hundred cows then owned by the Hays family, twenty-five had lifetime milk production records of 100,000 pounds. No other privately owned dairy herd in Canada was its equal at that time.

Some recognition of the quality of the Hays herd was given in February 1945, when the Holstein-Friesian Association of Canada, at its annual meeting in Toronto, presented Hays with its Master Breeder's Award.

□   □   □

Before he made his move into politics, Harry Hays was famous not just for his skill as a cattle breeder. Almost purely by chance, he had also become one of North America's top livestock auctioneers.

In his 1965 *Star Weekly* interview with Walter Stewart, he said it started one day in 1948 when he was managing a cattle sale, and the auctioneer hired for the occasion took sick. Hays stepped into the breach and, Stewart reported, "he was an instant success."

His brother Jack remembered it differently. The Hays brothers were having a cattle sale at Oakville one day, and the auctioneer was Lorne E. Franklin, considered one of Canada's best. At one point that day, Franklin told the Hays brothers, "You're not paying me enough; you're going to have to pay me more money." Tom, Harry and Jack went out behind the barn for a tactical huddle. They decided they were not going to pay Franklin any more money.

"So we started to try to sell behind the barn. Just like you were selling that post there. See who could get the most out of it. We were going to sell that sale. We weren't going to give in to this auctioneer. Harry, he was the best—that's what we thought. We voted on him. So that's how he got started. We weren't dependent on that auctioneer any more."

Back in Calgary, one of the auctioneers Hays teamed up with was his childhood friend from Carstairs, Archie Boyce. He was thirteen or fourteen years older than Hays—he had been taught in Carstairs school by Hays's mother—and was already a veteran of auctioneering on farms all over Alberta. Boyce remembered that he and Hays sold some 300,000 head of cattle at the Calgary stockyards one year. "That would be typical. Harry handled the largest Jersey sale, the largest consignment sale and the largest dispersal and sold a Jersey female for a record $10,600 in 1955." Hays did not sell as many farm sales as Boyce did; he preferred the big sales in cities and towns. Along with having fun, Boyce and Hays both made good livings for those days from their auctioneering. In the 1940s Boyce used to make $30,000 a year, and Hays earned even more.

Boyce believed auctioneering had stood Hays in good stead for his later political career. "You get to know people; pretty well tell what people are going to do when they're standing there bidding. Are they going to quit or keep on going? You've got to size this up."

They both developed some talent as actors. "You had to keep putting on a little act or they wouldn't pay any attention to you. You kidded them along and told jokes. It was a kind of an act. It's not so much that way today—more mechanical, like robots. . . . The other auctioneers never got write-ups like we did. Wherever we went there would be reporters."

A 1955 news clipping called him and Hays the Johnny Wayne and Frank Shuster of auctioneering. An unidentified 1954 clipping about one of their Calgary performances read: "It almost looked as if auctioneers Archie Boyce and Harry Hays were injecting a little religion into the cattle business (not that cattlemen are less religious than any other group of Albertans) at the annual spring bull sale." The crowd in the livestock pavilion, where Boyce and Hays were selling Aberdeen Angus bulls, found themselves barraged with "hallelujahs."

Unable to get what he considered a fair price for one animal, Archie apologized to the seller. Hays, in a pitying voice, informed the crowd that the seller's brother was out in the barns crying. "Why, brother," said Boyce, "we should all be crying, having to sell good bulls this low. Let us bow our heads. This is a sad occasion." The clipping reported: "From there the thing snowballed and for a few minutes the pavilion took on all the aspects of a good old-fashioned revival meeting." But there was no divine intervention; the average price of the bulls was only $378 each, compared to $443 the year before.

Hays by then enjoyed travelling by air as much as by any other means. Boyce recalled:

We were going up one time to a sale at Marwayne, up in north-eastern Alberta. We hired a fellow with a small plane to fly us in there. We left Calgary in the morning. It was a beautiful morning. By golly, when we got up north of Lacombe, turning off to fly east, we ran into a fog and we got lost up there. We couldn't see a thing. The pilot didn't know where we were.

Harry was a Catholic. He said, "You goddamn Protestants better start talking to the Lord. Looks like we're going to have it here." Finally somebody spotted a grain elevator through the fog. The pilot dropped down and flew around so we could get a better look at the elevator, and it said Kitscoty. We were able to figure then it was on the railroad to Lloydminster, not too far east. So we started in the direction the railway was going, east to Lloydminster, and we got down and were all right. But it looked pretty bad for a while. Harry got quite a kick out of this.

Like other long-time friends, Boyce remembered Hays's love of practical jokes. In 1955, when Boyce was running for election on a Liberal ticket, the pair had an auction together. Hays got up to test the loudspeaking system, and he kept saying over it: "Vote Social Credit. Vote Social Credit."

I remember one time we were in Medicine Hat. We came in from this sale, got into the motel, took off our clothes mostly, sitting around in our shorts. It was nice weather. We had a meal sent in. When we got through with this meal, Harry said, "What are we going to do with these plates?" I said, "Oh, we'll take them out and put them on top of the car." So I went out. And Harry locked the door. Well, he was looking out the window laughing to bust a gut. He wouldn't let me back in for quite a while. I couldn't very well go and get another key.

Boyce could get his own back now and then.

One time we went to Toronto for the Royal Winter Fair. We happened to be on different floors at the hotel. Some of these western people who knew me phoned on a Sunday and said, "Do you know where I can get a bottle?" Several of them phoned me. I gave them

Harry's room. I said, "He does a little bit of bootlegging in the hotel." But I said, "Don't phone him until midnight." By this time Harry was in bed. Next day Harry said, "I don't know what the hell was going on last night. They started phoning me asking if I had any booze to sell." . . . Finally he tumbled.

Calgary businessman and gentleman farmer Ed O'Connor was one of Hays's closest friends. They met when Hays joined the downtown Calgary Rotary Club in 1941 for the purpose of widening his business contacts. They also served together on the Calgary Stampede board of directors, and O'Connor was later a manager of Hays's federal election campaigns. Like Archie Boyce, he remembered the mischief in the man along with the brilliance and flare. As secretary of their Rotary Club when Hays was president, O'Connor remembered that pranks found their way into club affairs, too.

I remember one time he was trying to get a vote through on the Rotary Club auctioning a house. There was nip and tuck feeling amongst the members. So Harry in his inimitable way said, "All right, now; we're going to take a vote, and those of you who are opposed to it, stand up and face the wall." Needless to say, the vote went over with a great majority. That was Harry Hays. Harry never put life aside.

As an auctioneer, O'Connor remembered, "Hays was fantastic. He was unusual. He was a fellow that you had to watch very carefully because he picked up your least motion, particularly of a friend. I remember one incident when a fellow Rotarian walked into the ring, and he sort of raised his hand. Harry said, 'Sold!' The fellow said, 'Now what the hell do I do with a calf?' " But Hays never took a practical joke too far. "He always followed it through; if you wished, he got rid of the animal for you."

Under a heading "So you are going to have a sale," Hays offered blunt but tactful advice in an August 1958 article in the *Holstein-Friesian Journal:*

If a man wants to sell his cattle at home, sometimes on the way to see him or on the way home, I ask his neighbors, "What kind of fel-

low is this man Brown?" If you get a reception like this, and sometimes you do, "Why, that cheapskate is tighter than hair on a dog's
back"—or "He's meaner than all get out"—or the neighbor's wife
says, "I'd hate to meet him on the road with a flat tire," you can just
bet these people are not going to help the sale too much.

So it is important for your sale that your place is neat, well taken
care of and prosperous looking and that your neighbors will help.
Otherwise, it is best to move your cattle where they can stand on
their merits alone. Sell your machinery at home and pray for the
best. . . . Whatever you do, don't lie about your cows. . . . [and]
don't be a crybaby interrupting the sales force.

Above all, he concluded, start exactly on time: "Don't wait for
buyers you think should have come. The ones that are on time
came to buy."

In 1950 Hays pioneered at Lethbridge the selling of cattle by
auction at public stockyards, a practice to this day followed across
Canada and the United States. Until then farmers selling their cattle
had dealt with commission agencies or representatives of meat
packers, often as a result getting paid less than better-informed
neighbours.

Hays's auctioneering services eventually enjoyed a wide demand,
and he sold some of the best cattle for many of the best breeders in
every province excepting Newfoundland. In Quebec he did his auctioneering through interpreters when French was called for. He
also auctioned purebred cattle for clients in twenty-eight states. At
his peak he estimated that he was the auctioneer for 60 per cent of
the Jersey sales in North America and 90 per cent of the Holstein
sales in Canada. A list of his clientele read like someone's blue
book: he auctioned off purebreds for General Motors president
Charles Wilson, for Toronto millionaire E. P. Taylor, for Toronto's
Massey family, for another Toronto millionaire, Steve Roman, and
for Alberta millionaire J. B. Cross. To mention a few.

During this time Hays—often accompanied by Muriel—travelled
an average of 35,000 miles each year (always first class where
available) and auctioned several million dollars' worth of cattle
every year. He could earn as much as $5,000 for a single day's
work. On one occasion, while selling at the Lethbridge stockyards,

Hays sold $109,000 worth of cattle in twenty-seven minutes, an auctioneering record at that time. He could sell as many as two thousand head of cattle in a single day.

At an auction in California during the late 1940s, Hays sold the world's most expensive cow, and he often told the story. He arrived in town a day or so before he was to do his selling stint, and he went back into the barns to have a look at a cow which he knew was the best he would be handling this sale. A man came up beside him, looked at the cow and then asked Hays what he thought she might sell for. Hays responded deadpan with a figure he just grabbed from the air. "Oh," he supposed, "maybe eighteen, twenty thousand dollars." Showing no evident surprise, the man stared thoughtfully at Hays, murmured something and left.

A few minutes later another man came up and put a similar question. This time Hays considered and then replied, "Well, she might go as high as twenty-two, twenty-five thousand." Nor did this prospective buyer seem shocked at such a possible price.

When Hays started auctioning the cow before a large crowd in a tent the next day, the first man was one of the eager bidders. The cow's price quickly ran up to $28,000, then to $29,000. Hays paused and looked deep into the man's eyes. The man stared back. A hush fell across the crowd. Then the man made what turned out to be the final bid and bought the cow for $33,000.

"And of course," Hays would say, "the minute she sold for that price, she was worth it, and probably more, for all the publicity she'd get and the price increase for her offspring that would come of it."

Years later, after he had become a senator, Hays far surpassed that and all the other cattle auctioneering records. On 8 November 1976 he took a day off from the Senate to play his familiar role of auctioneer at the "Sale of Stars," which he introduced to Toronto's Royal Winter Fair in 1952. One of the animals he sold was a Holstein named Hanover Hill Barb (VG). She brought a world record price of $235,000.

CHAPTER SIX

MAKING
A NEW
BREED

Ed O'Connor spoke of the visionary element in Harry Hays's makeup. "He was a trailblazer. Harry was the type of fellow who said, 'Well, everybody says it won't work, but nobody's tried it.' He had thoughts sometimes when you were sitting down talking with him; you'd say, 'Hell, man, you've fallen out of your tree,' because his thoughts were so much ahead of your own thinking. But after you'd spent a little bit of time with Harry, you'd start thinking, 'Well, this is not quite as ridiculous as it first appeared to be.' He had great vision and he had the courage of his visions."

O'Connor remembered as perhaps the best example of both Hays's vision and his tenacity in the pursuit of it, the development around 1957 of a new purebred breed of beef cattle—Hays's own breed. He recalled how often Hays talked about the work he was doing on his breed. "After five or seven years you'd say, 'Hell, man, you've got yourself up against a brick wall. How are you going to get through it?' He'd say, 'I'll get through it. I'll make it.' "

By 1957 Hays had completed the sale for real estate development purposes of all but the old family house, the barn and about seventeen acres of the dairy farm, by then a part of Calgary's expanding southern suburbs. He had invested a substantial portion of the proceeds in his ranch southwest of Calgary. The ranch fields were in a large, shallow valley, mostly flat and highly suitable for raising cattle and grain. Just beyond the western fences, the land rose in soaring foothills of the Rocky Mountains. It was well-watered land—Pekisko and Stimson creeks flowed through it, creating a couple of large ponds which, as a hobby, Hays kept well stocked with trout for eating now and then as a change from beef.

The idea for a new beef breed had been gestating a long time in Hays's mind. As an auctioneer selling everything from purebred cattle and sheep to horses and hogs, he gradually became aware that beef animals had evolved in a direction opposite to consumers' demands. Hog breeders had moved towards leaner animals that produced less fat while beef breeders had concentrated on fat animals. "One day we'd be selling cattle and have to say, look how thick, look how deep, look how short and low to the ground. The next day we'd be selling hogs and be talking about how long and lean and upstanding they were. It just didn't make sense. We were selling lard cattle long after they found nobody wanted lard-type hogs."

Besides wanting to develop a lean-meated breed of cow, Hays wanted one that gained weight as efficiently as genes would allow. He aimed at developing an animal that would reach the preferred marketable weight at the earliest possible age. He drew his reasoning from the observation of human babies.

Take a baby with a genetic potential to be about 165 pounds at maturity. When it's born it weighs about 8 pounds and in a year gains over 17 pounds. All the rest of his life, he'll never convert food as efficiently as he does in that first year. The second year, he weighs maybe 35 pounds but eats twice as much. In each succeeding year, he gains less, eats more and therefore is a less efficient converter of food into growth.

Relating this to the cattle business, Hays said there was one major figure to work towards. The market demanded a steer in the magic range of 1100 pounds. His goal, then, for maximum economic benefit, was to breed a beef animal that would reach this desirable market weight during its first year of life, when it could most efficiently convert feed to meat. "The more efficiently they convert feed to meat, the younger you can get them to 1100 pounds—and to market."

Hays explained that the potential for the offspring of a 1000-pound sire and a 700-pound dam did not interest him. "The most efficient conversion you'll get from the progeny will be when they're only about 200 pounds. Everything after that will be put on at a less and less efficient rate." However, if a 3000-pound bull were mated with a 1300-pound cow, "the magic figure of 1100 pounds will be reached at a younger age by the progeny, and therefore the gains will be both faster and more efficient."

By that time Hays had perhaps more personal experience with farming to draw on for guidance in his quest than almost any farmer in Canada. Not only had he his experience as president of the Canadian Swine Breeders during the 1940s and as an auctioneer for two decades; he knew from his experience as president of the Alberta Poultry Breeders' Association and as a chicken breeder that much the same thing was happening with chickens.

A broiler chicken producer at Galt, Ontario, Donald McQ. Shaver, had begun to take advantage of the fact that chicks, like human babies, convert food to growth most efficiently in the earliest period of existence. During the first third of their twelve-week maturization period, chicks produce more edible meat from less feed than at any other time in their lives. Shaver had mated a ten-pound rooster with an eight-pound hen—both enormous birds in the chicken world. His goal was a broiler that could mature to three pounds in twelve weeks at a conversion rate of two pounds of feed to one pound of meat—a goal Hays knew Shaver had achieved.

"He broke the purebred registration myth," Hays said. "He didn't want an identified breed in which bad qualities could be locked in. He sold birds strictly on their performance." This was what Hays set out to do with beef cattle—develop an animal that would be measured solely on its performance as a converter of feed to salable meat, not on appearance, colour, width between the eyes, tail settings, depth of flank, or carcass marbling, though these were factors most other beef producers still paid much attention to. In the language of the farm trade, he wanted to breed up a cow with hardiness against Canadian winters, fast fleshing ability and calving ease, "growthiness," large milk production for her calves and a trouble-free udder. He also wanted her to have a high fertility rate, good legs and feet, and an excellent carcass.

From his experience as a dairy farmer, Hays knew that a calf needed plenty of milk from its mother to ensure maximum growth. Yet farm experience also showed him that the average beef cow does not produce a sustained supply of milk for her calf after the initial heavy flow at the beginning of lactation. Aware that it required about nine pounds of milk to produce one pound of meat in an average calf, Hays began the evolution of his new beef animal by mixing dairy and beef cattle.

Hays also knew that line breeding, or incest, would be essential to his task, and he often joked about this with journalists. He would remind them that he was a Roman Catholic and so took seriously the biblical adjurations against inbreeding, incest, marrying cousins or other close blood relatives. "These precautions might have been good guidelines for the preservation of nomadic peoples who wrote the Bible, but in cattle genetics they have no place. I mated the best families, father to daughter, son to mother, and other such incestuous combinations to bring out the best meat-producing characteristics possible. Look at Cleopatra—she was the result of four brother-sister matings and an uncle and a niece, and we're still talking about her two thousand years later."

Hays started his evolutionary quest by carefully combining progeny from three outstanding animals, each from a different existing breed. Spring Farm Fond Hope was a Holstein bull weighing 3120 pounds and famous in agricultural circles for producing daughters that were large, yet more meaty than most other Holstein cows. Silver Prince 7P was a 2400-pound Hereford bull noted for his ability to transmit size, length, bone and fleshing ability to his offspring. Jane of Vernon was a 1600-pound Brown Swiss cow famous for having what was judged the world's most perfect udder.

Hays selected eight sons of dairy bull Fond Hope to mate in the autumn of 1957 with his neighbouring rancher James Allen Baker's herd of large Hereford beef cows and arranged to buy all the calves produced. From them and successive generations, Hays would select only those bulls that weighed at least 1100 pounds at one year of age; a bull's worth also was measured by the number of offspring that stayed in the herd over the following years. Cows, too, were initially selected for their growth performance. But once in the brood herd, their selection depended on their ability to both produce offspring and survive. Every one of them had to have a calf annually to remain in the herd; each one had to become pregnant from the bull's first service, and she had to have the calf unassisted in the open pasture; if she had any trouble with the birth, or with the nursing of her calf once safely born, or needed help in any other way—hoof trimming, for example, or milking out—her tail was bobbed to mark her, and she was shipped off to the slaughterhouse come autumn.

Hays preferred to graze his animals on minimal pasture to keep them lean and hungry. "When stress is placed on any species and survival becomes a fact of life, the natural instinct is to breed for preservation. This is the method I use to assure a high fertility rate in the breed. If you can't get a cow bred, she's just a boarder, and you lose money on her."

The evolutionary law of survival of the fittest was followed ruthlessly. Hays insisted that each cow produce a good supply of milk from the Holstein genes in her body. He believed that the two most important things in cows were wombs and udders—having accessible and reliable feeding teats would enable the new Hays animal to survive winters outside much more comfortably.

"My Converter cattle have udders comparable to a woman of eighty who still doesn't need to wear a bra," Hays would say. "They supply plenty of milk to the calves near the end of lactation when the calves need it most for growth." But neither did he want too much. He did not want to have to milk any of his cows because they produced more milk than their calves could drink. Hays especially admired the qualities of Jane of Vernon. "In addition to having the most perfect udder, she never ever had her feet trimmed. We really chose her, though, because she peaked in her milk production in her eighth month. I'd seen too many cows fall off completely in their milk just as their calves got big enough to utilize it all. I wanted a cow that would peak later in her production, and Jane of Vernon, through her offspring, did just that."

Two years later the best females born from these matings, granddaughters of Fond Hope, were bred to Silver Prince. Five of the best bulls from these matings, sons of Silver Prince and great-grandsons of Fond Hope, were selected to mate with their mothers, Fond Hope's granddaughters produced by the original matings with Baker's Herefords. Having thus brought together in unholy incestuousness the specially gifted progeny of Fond Hope and Silver Prince, Hays next introduced the superior genetics of Jane of Vernon's offspring, with their tidy-teated udders. He mated four of her great-grandsons with one hundred Hereford cows. The female progeny from these encounters were then put into the breeding herd; now that Hays had combined the genetic materials he wanted, the herd was closed to all other outside breeding influence. By 1969 his own breed of cows had been bred to his own breed of bulls regularly and exclusively for seven years, and his work on improving nature's genetics was producing the results he had anticipated. The animal he called the Hays Converter—most of them black with white faces, but some of them red with white faces—was proving to be the fastest gaining beef beast in North America.

The previous year he had put five of his bulls into the government beef testing station at Bassano, Alberta. Their weight gain per day was measured against that of animals from conventional British-based beef breeds, as well as from the more recently imported French Charolais beef breed, over the same period of time and on the same feed. The Hays bulls averaged one-third more daily gain than the British-breed bulls and registered an average feed conversion of 5.98 pounds of feed for each pound of weight gained. Only three Charolais bulls had better conversion rates than the Hays Converters, but none of them came close to the record of his best individual bull in the testing station, which had put on weight at a rate of 3.96 pounds each day.

"Our Converter steers are going to market in June and July," Hays announced at that time. They would have reached the preferred market weight of 1000 to 1100 pounds by the time they were thirteen or fourteen months old, whereas Herefords on Hays's ranch would not reach that weight until they were eighteen or nineteen months old. "The Converters have only attained about 55 per cent of their growth by the time they're ready for market," Hays proudly pointed out. "When the Herefords go out in November, December and even January, they have reached about 85 per cent of their growth, and their feed-to-meat conversion rate has been getting worse all the time."

The average parentage weight of the Hays Converters was 1800 pounds, compared to 1300 pounds for the Herefords on his ranch. "We get double the milk production with our cows," Hays explained, "and this production peaks two months after calving, instead of right at calving. Nine pounds of milk will give a pound of meat, so a cow that will give 1000 pounds more milk will give you over 100 pounds more calf, and we end up with a big husky calf in the fall. No matter how well the British breeds convert after that, they can never catch up."

Gainability and milk production were not the only reasons Hays had mixed Hereford and Holstein genetics in his Converter. "If you just want gainability, nothing can compete with straight Holsteins. But we get a more acceptable beef carcass by adding Hereford blood. They finish out well at 1000 to 1100 pounds—ideal packer weight—while you have to feed straight Holsteins to 1300 or 1400 pounds." In 1969 he could boast: "We've been getting $320 to $340 apiece for our Converter steers, which is better than some bulls bring at the purebred sales. They cost us less and we sell them for more, so what are these other fellas in business for, anyway?"

Underlying Hays's claims were the detailed results of 1967–68 beef animal feed-gain testing in government-supervised stations across Canada. The Hays Converter had topped the 537 animals tested. Its average daily weight gain of 3.68 pounds in the 140-day test compared with 3.41 pounds for the next best, the Charolais, 2.71 for Hereford, 2.54 for Galloway, 2.39 for Aberdeen Angus and 2.29 for Shorthorn. At the age of one year the Converter weighed an average 1135 pounds, Charolais 1079, Hereford 890, Galloway 877, Aberdeen Angus 855 and Shorthorn 882.

In following years the Converter continued to lead in weight-gain performance. From 1970 through 1982, Hays Converter bulls in federal-provincial performance tests weighed an average of 1086 pounds at the age of one year. This was 233 pounds more than the 853-pound average for all breeds during that time. "The reason is no secret," Hays would say. "They've been bred to do it."

Hays could also point out the practical cost-savings in producing a faster-gaining beef animal. If feed cost $60 a ton, an animal gaining three and a half pounds a day would make that growth at a cost of 18 cents a pound. An animal gaining only two pounds a day from the same amount of feed would cost 36.5 cents per pound of growth, and the cost for an animal gaining only a pound a day would be 63 cents per pound of growth. "Why," Hays would ask, "spend 63 cents to put a pound of gain on an animal when it is only going to bring 30 cents live weight at the marketplace?"

In June 1969 American Breeders Service, a Wisconsin-based worldwide distributor of livestock semen for artificial insemination, announced an exclusive arrangement with Hays for the marketing of Hays Converter semen. Initially semen would be available from three Converter bulls named Tom, Dick and Harry. Hays announced that he would not sell any of the offspring of his new breed for breeding purposes, but would only sell semen and lease bulls.

Cattle breeding history was made at the Hays ranch on 23 October 1969 before some 750 persons from every Canadian province, thirteen American states including Hawaii, and England, Scotland, France, Australia and the Caribbean. The occasion was the official unveiling at a field day jointly organized by Hays and the American Breeders Service of the Hays Converter, though it had yet to win official recognition as a registered purebred breed.

The Edmonton *Journal* reported that "Georgia stockmen in blue toques mingled excitedly with bearded Hutterites in sombre black hats and Montana cowboys in white Stetsons to see Hays's revolutionary, multi-colored cattle—which thumbs its nose at conventional breed standards." The agriculture editor of London's *Financial Times* and a CBC television crew were also present. Several planeloads of cattlemen had flown into Calgary from the United States and had taken buses to the ranch. The day was chilly, and four inches of snow had fallen in Calgary, but the storm did not reach the ranch until evening. By then all the visitors had had plenty of opportunity both to look over the new Hays animals and to savour their flavour—the visitors were served about seven hundred pounds of barbecued Converter beef.

The publicity helped to widen interest in the Hays Converter across the international agricultural community. Not every breeder shared Hays's enthusiasm by a long shot, however. Those attached to the more traditional British-based beef breeds were sometimes especially critical of the look of the Converter. Hays having deliberately bred it to have less belly fat, the Converter's belly noticeably hung several inches higher off the ground than did its Hereford associates'. Vague references to criticisms of the Converter frequently found their way into news stories.

Canadian Cattlemen magazine had reported in June 1968: "When the Hays project began back in 1957 . . . about the only people who weren't outright scoffers at the time were a few feed salesmen who had watched Mr. Hays feed out fast-gaining crossbred Holstein steers and the packer buyers who had seen the carcasses hung up." One of Hays's neighbouring ranchers was quoted as saying: "Oh, those half-Holstein cows of Harry Hays will wean heavier calves, all right. But they're so damn thin by fall they have an awful time coming through the winter."

A *Canadian Cattlemen* reporter decided to see for himself. After viewing Converters and Herefords that had grazed out all winter with no supplementary feed, he reported: "They all looked much the same; pretty thin, but strong and healthy and all producing calves." Hays, it was pointed out, did not believe in overfeeding cattle during the winter. He once told a neighbour who had fed seventy cows over the winter that he should have had twice that many for all that feed. "There's no use running a fat cow," Hays said. "The only thing she can do is to wean a calf in the fall. If you have more feed, give it to more cattle, instead of making fewer of them fat."

Alberta brewery millionaire and purebred Hereford breeder J. B. Cross thought the Hays Converter about the ugliest cattle beast he had ever laid eyes on. Similar comments from livestock traditionalists neither surprised nor particularly bothered Hays since, as he pointed out in a *Time* interview in 1968, producing a lean beef animal, just as hog producers had been doing, was precisely what he had intended. He would chuckle, "We decided to produce a pig of a cow."

Hays's beef breeding dream achieved fruition on 4 December 1975, when the first purebred Certificate of Registration was issued for his Converter by the Canadian National Livestock Records under provisions of the Livestock Pedigree Act. By early 1985 there were ninety-five listed herds of registered Hays Converters—eight-seven in seven provinces and eight in five American states.

CHAPTER SEVEN

SEASONING IN OFFICE

By 1959, the year of Harry Hays's mayoralty campaign, he and Muriel had become famous around Calgary for the warm informality of their particular brand of homey hospitality. It had begun with having potential customers for Hays cattle over for a drink and a sandwich. Now they frequently held a combination cocktail party–buffet supper at their spacious home, often inviting substantial numbers of guests. Frequently they would have two parties, one one night and the other the following night for those who could not attend the first night.

"He loved to be with people," Hays's long-time Rotary colleague Charlie Kennedy recalled. "He and his wife entertained every member of the Rotary Club and their wives during his term as president in 1958. Thirty or forty people at a time. He cooked these tremendous prime roasts of beef. They were famous for it." The bar was always well stocked, and the liquor flowed generously in keeping with the habit of the times. Beans were served along with the beef. Although the Hayses had hired help with the catering, they cooked their own meat because, as Muriel said, "we liked the way we cooked it better. You'd take a pound a person. You wouldn't get a thirty-pound roast. You can cook three twelve-to-fifteen-pound roasts in an oven. Instead of putting them flat, stand them up. It doesn't take any longer than cooking one."

After Hays became mayor, they would entertain the whole council and their spouses once a month in this same way. Grant MacEwan's wife, Phyllis, used to play the Hayses' piano while others stood around it and sang.

By then, as well, the Hays Stampede breakfast was becoming famous. According to Hays, the breakfast that is now a tradition on the first Sunday morning of the Calgary Stampede began almost by chance. In July of 1952 he and Arthur Crawford-Frost, a southern Alberta Hereford breeder who was president of the Stampede that year, invited a large number of friends to breakfast on the spacious, tree-shaded lawns at the Hays home the Sunday before the Stampede opened. At that time the Stampede began on a Monday morning with a huge parade; the breakfast would be a warm-up party. (Now it opens the Friday morning before the Hays breakfast.) As is still done today, they served gin and grapefruit juice, scrambled eggs and sausages, fried potatoes, toast and coffee, starting about 6:30 A.M.

Everyone had such a good time that Hays and two business associates who were also fellow Rotary members, owner Watson Hook of Hook Signs and Ron Jenkins of the western grocery-chain family, decided to do it again the next year. They planned a relatively small, private get-together, inviting a few personal friends and business associates.

Jenkins, however, was at a large party that Friday night and became so filled with spirits of generosity that he invited virtually everyone present to the Sunday morning breakfast. Instead of the couple of dozen persons expected, the breakfasting celebrants swelled to about three hundred, and included former world heavyweight boxing champion Jack Dempsey. But everyone again had such a good time that, year after year, Hays and his partners went on holding the breakfast, inviting more and more people and adding more and more entertainments to the agenda, until the Hays breakfast had become a widely famed Stampede tradition—one still carried on by Hays's son, Dan, and several partners.

□   □   □

Harry Hays told several versions, usually amusing, of how, in October 1959, he came to run for the office of mayor of Calgary without any experience in politics and without having shown any obvious signs of caring about a political career. The main thread running through all of these stories begins with the fact that by 1959, Hays's successes in farming, auctioneering, and in the sale of the valuable suburban Calgary real estate that the old family dairy farm had become, had put him in such a comfortable financial position that, at the age of forty-nine, he was thinking of retiring. Then some friends, unhappy with the incumbent city government, urged him to run for alderman and help clean up the situation. Or perhaps he himself planned the idea with his friends, and *then* they asked him. It is even possible that he only made up being asked at all.

Years later Hays spoke of a prominent Albertan who had complained to him that he would have run in an election for the Liberals if someone had only asked him to. "Hell," Hays said, "that's not how you get into politics. You don't hang around waiting for somebody to ask you, and do it all for you. I knew exactly what I wanted. I decided to get into politics because I wanted to be mayor. And I knew damn well I'd have to run on my own if I wanted to be sure of doing it. I had to want it more than anybody else wanted it for me. It just don't work any other way in politics."

Once it began to spread among his friends, the idea of Harry Hays running for civic alderman's office was accepted and supported. However, as the idea caught on, it also grew, at least in Hays's own mind, for it occurred to him that he might only be frustrated as an alderman: "I thought, what the hell; if I was going to run, I'd shoot the bundle."

My wife and I were driving down to our ranch, and they were trying to get somebody to run against this fellow in office [Don Mackay]. We were driving down just about three weeks before the election. I said to my wife, "You know, I think I'll run for mayor." "Oh, God,

Harry," she said, "you couldn't get that job, and if you did, you couldn't run the city." Now that was kind of a challenge to me. So about a week or ten days after that, I decided to run.

The idea was tested around the city and met with much enthusiasm. Muriel later said: "Harry had some plans he thought Calgary could stand. He thought there were a lot of things that could be done in Calgary that weren't being done. He thought he'd like to see if he could get them done."

Dan Hays was not entirely sure it was only an urge to change things that motivated his father.

> He ran for mayor when he was forty-nine. He'd been doing something for a long time. Whether you're successful at it or not, at that age you start looking around and say to yourself, what could I do that's more interesting? I suspect that was an element. He never said this, but if he had stayed in federal politics, I'm sure he would have been one of those who would have been anxious to be the leader of the party. He was ambitious.

The man Hays had to beat to become mayor, Don Mackay, was a personal acquaintance who, with his wife, was frequently a dinner guest at the Hays home. Even before Hays decided to run against Mackay, there was talk around Calgary about Mackay's accepting construction aid for a Banff cottage on questionable, if not slightly scandalous, grounds. Not long before he decided to run for mayor, Hays forbade discussion of the subject in his presence. He did not approve of scandalmongering. Nevertheless, it became one of the issues in the civic election campaign; by then an inquiry had reprimanded Mackay for using his mayor's position to improper advantage.

According to Jack Hays, it is possible that Mackay unwittingly challenged Hays to run against him. "Harry knew Don Mackay very well. But Don didn't believe what Harry believed. He thought that Harry was wrong on a lot of things, and Harry thought, well, I'll prove it to him."

One of the first persons Hays called when he did make up his mind to run for mayor was Arthur Smith, the Progressive Conservative M.P. for Calgary South. They were long-time acquaintances through various activities carried out as supporters of the Calgary Chamber of Commerce and the Calgary Stampede. Smith always consulted Hays in particular when he needed any advice about agricultural matters.

Smith remembered it was a Sunday. "He phoned me. His style was so direct. There was never any grey area with Harry. He said, 'Art, are you going to run as mayor?' I said no. He said, 'I am, and I need your help.'" So Smith took the job of Hays's campaign manager.

Calgary *Herald* columnist Merv Anderson was the city hall reporter that year. He had first met Hays in 1956, when he'd been sent out to the dairy farm to interview Hays, who was then president of the downtown Calgary Rotary Club. Anderson had gone prepared to be bored, but it turned out to be the beginning of a long friendship.

"He was a genial, hospitable guy, very much the Rotarian. I was pretty impressed with the place and the hospitality. I warmed up to him. I liked the smile. He was a shy guy but came across as an extrovert."

Like Smith, Anderson was surprised when Hays decided to run for mayor. "Other than service club activity, he had no background in civic affairs. He had never been in city hall before, literally." But both seem to have been taken by Hays's refreshing, if blunt, candour and almost naive integrity.

"All people who run for political office are inclined to say that they want to make a contribution to the community," Smith said. "I think this with Harry was probably very real. He didn't do it for money. He didn't do it for prestige; he already had the recognition as a cattle breeder. So one has to just believe him that he wanted to make a contribution."

Charlie Kennedy, the long-time manager of the Calgary stockyards, both collected and contributed money for Hays's first campaign and wrote some material for it. Hays ran on a simple platform of "working together" for a better Calgary. One sentence in his campaign pamphlet revealed his underlying political naiveté: "Harry Hays believes in working for the elimination of politics in any form in our civic administration."

Alderman P. N. R. Morrison had served on Calgary city council for fourteen years before Hays ran for the mayor's job. He remembered it as a very close race—and a bitter one for defending Mayor Don Mackay and his loyal supporters. "Mackay got more votes in defeat than he ever did in victory." (He won 33,562, just 1484 fewer than the 35,046 that elected Hays mayor on 14 October 1959.) "Hays's home received so many derogatory and inflammatory phone calls that he bought two Dobermans following his election as mayor. That was indication to me that he had some pretty fierce opponents in town. I don't think Mackay's supporters ever came around."

Hays's sister Laura, then living in Vancouver, received a phone call from him right after his election win. "He said, 'When am I supposed to officially take office?' I said, 'God, I don't know. Why don't you ask your campaign manager, Art Smith?' He says, 'I don't want him to know I don't know.' That was Harry." Later he joked that the mayor's office was so plush, he had had to take in a lawnmower to mow the rug because it was so deep he could not move around.

Friends like Grant MacEwan, already a Calgary alderman for several years when Hays was first elected, were surprised at how little trouble Hays had learning his role as chairman of city council. This, of course, overlooked the years of experience he had already chalked up as a chairman of various farm organization meetings, Rotary, chamber of commerce and Stampede committees—not to mention the unique public-speaking experiences available to auctioneers.

"Hays came into council chambers as a breath of fresh air," MacEwan recalled. "He was untried as an administrator, and he was handicapped by inexperience, but Harry never lacked courage. He bluffed his way through very effectively. He was stepping into the big league." But Hays's supposed inexperience was not a handicap, nor were his council meetings a shambles. "Nearly everybody was glad to see him there. Certainly nearly everybody on council had a welcome for him because they had been very critical of Mackay."

Alderman Morrison had always considered it one of his responsibilities to view all that went on at city hall with a critical, if not jaundiced, eye. He was as critical of Hays during his tenure as he had been of Mackay during his, though Hays never held that against him. Morrison remembered Hays as a very friendly person. "He wasn't on council very long before he had everyone eating out of his hand. He presided over the city council with dignity, a pleasant dignity. There were no great noisy scenes while he was mayor. That's a benefit to the city." (When he was a federal minister, Hays said of being mayor: "I was chairman, Speaker of the House and every other damn thing. It wasn't like Parliament at all.")

Hays admitted, years later, that he deliberately meant not to effect very much in the way of policy making during his first few months in office, to give himself a chance to size up the civic situation thoroughly. This soon began to arouse some criticism that he was a do-nothing mayor. But Hays did not let that bother him. "Once you do start to do things, the critics forget about the time you didn't do anything, as long as what you do do, once you start, you get right. But if you start off too soon and you make a mistake or two, then the critics never forget. They'll be rubbing your nose in it for years to come."

One of the first controversial decisions Hays made was to revolutionize the rules of city council meetings. He quickly grew tired and impatient at having to preside over council sessions that often rambled on for eight or ten hours far into the night. He persuaded his fellow council members to accept a five-minute limit on speeches, and then as chairman of the meetings he enforced the limit with a cheerful rigorousness that sometimes enraged the long-winded. But for the rest of Hays's reign as mayor, council meetings seldom lasted more than a couple of hours.

Hays also changed the style of mayoring in Calgary. His flamboyant predecessor's trademark had been a white Stetson always worn in public. Hays let the white cowboy hat continue to be a symbol of Calgary's western heritage and the Stampede, but he did not stop wearing the narrow-brimmed cattleman's hat he had always worn. He also cut back on the social life of the mayor. Mackay had loved the social activities that went with the position; Hays preferred to devote his time to the business of city hall, and often delegated other council members to represent him at social occasions. The Calgary *Herald* reported, as Hays approached his second mayoralty campaign, that he had attended a minimum of tea parties. But if he could be criticized for missing too many social engagements, "he has been in his office every morning at 7:30." He later told columnist Charles Lynch, "You've got to be tough. We run the city like a bank or the CPR. The day starts at 7:30 A.M., and we hold our first meeting at a quarter to eight."

Muriel Hays said her husband had never been a good sleeper, and this led him to do a lot of his reading during the night hours. Or he would start his day early. His Calgary friend Ed O'Connor recalled how Hays put this habit to use after he became mayor. "Harry was a 5 to 5:30 A.M. riser. When people would phone him and complain about something, Harry would phone them back about 6 A.M. and say, 'I hear you have a complaint. Would you like to pass it on to me now?' Complainants decided to drift away because it got around that unless you were prepared to answer your phone at six in the morning and often earlier, don't complain to the mayor."

Hays had read about the way Napoleon once governed Paris, and he believed some of Napoleon's approaches could usefully be applied to the governing of Calgary. To eliminate intergovernmental bickering at ratepayers' expense and to ensure equality of public services throughout the entire greater Calgary urban area, Hays instituted a program for annexing adjoining independent communities such as Forest Lawn on Calgary's northeastern outskirts and Bowness on the northwestern. This aroused considerable angry opposition, mostly from the civic politicians in each community whose jobs were on the block. The opponents wanted to retain their independent municipal status and not be swallowed into Calgary. Hays persevered, presiding over months of controversial public meetings with a mixture of patience, humour, hard bluster and skilled bargaining.

"The political leaders of those areas were dead against annexation to Calgary," Art Smith recalled. "But as the residents began to appreciate the advantages of being amalgamated, it no longer was a problem." During this time, the head of the greater Toronto metropolitan government, Fred Gardiner, telephoned Hays and encouraged him to persist with his amalgamation program, so that as Calgary grew in the future, it could avoid the problems Toronto had with its surrounding municipalities.

Hays had also noted in his reading that Napoleon had designed the wagon-wheel traffic layout of Paris, whereby a series of thoroughfares led outward from the centre of the city like spokes extending from hub to rim. He thought a similar plan, especially one including provision for ring roads that would allow traffic to skirt around the city, would be good for Calgary, too, and set out to have one devised. One of the earliest results was the Sarcee Trail, around Calgary's western outskirts.

The chief commissioner when Hays was mayor was a skilled government administrator, former Calgary finance commissioner Dudley Batchelor. The two became great friends and, to a substantial extent, fellow conspirators in devising new policy ideas and ways to get them through—or over or around or behind the back of—council. Once, their private scheming almost got them shot.

According to Hays, both were out one afternoon walking along a hillside on the northwestern outskirts of Calgary high above the Bow River, privately checking out the lay of some of the land that would have to be expropriated for the Sarcee Trail. Suddenly a shot rang out. The startled pair looked up to see the proprietor of the land standing above them. Angry at the city's already publicized plans to take over some of his land, he had fired a warning shot from his .22-calibre rifle. Hays tried to persuade the man that his traffic plan was worth giving up the land for. Although the man fired no further shots, Hays was never sure how convincing he had been.

Hays and Batchelor worked well together. They understood each other, they liked each other and they complemented each other. Batchelor was outstanding as a planner; his job was to keep the machinery of civic government running, and he did that extremely well, leaving Hays with the imaginative work and the political challenge of winning public acceptance.

Hays had the advantage, too, of coming in as a new broom. The media found him attractive and interesting; they were kindly to him. The Calgary *Herald* in particular helped his career. The *Herald* had been critical of Mackay, and now it was going to back Hays politically and give him every opportunity to be a successful mayor.

Hays would often remember how pleased some of his business friends were with his efforts to implement a pay-as-you-go budget policy—and then how outraged some of them were when, with the impartiality on which he based his proud claim that "I do not play politics," he approved council plans to cut down trees in front of their expensive homes so that Elbow Drive could be widened to accommodate an increasing traffic flow.

The first commercial jet airliners were just being put into service when Hays was mayor. The noise of their engines while landing and taking off close to cities became a focal point of a major political issue. Environmentalists aroused strong public demand that new airports be built far from the city's outskirts to save residents from the harms of jetliner noise. While Hays was truly concerned about the potentially harmful effects of the noise, he was also determined to keep the Calgary airport where it was, as close to downtown as possible. He was especially determined to avoid in Calgary what was happening about the same time in Edmonton.

In a move aimed both at appeasing the environmentalists and at becoming the main national and international jetliner airport in Alberta, the City of Edmonton had arranged a supplement for its inadequate downtown airport. Edmonton had signed a deal with the federal Department of Transport for construction of a new airport some fifteen miles south of the city. It would be not only out of hearing distance of Edmonton but out of sight as well. Its longer runways would be to jetliner landing and takeoff specifications. But its long distance from downtown Edmonton would be a source of frustration for air travellers from the moment of its completion.

The Edmonton plans created a complex of problems for Hays because they focussed on the jet noise problem in Calgary, too. Calgary's airport would need substantial renovation and expansion if there were to be any serious hope of attracting away from Edmonton the lion's share of national and international traffic in the rapidly dawning jet age. Hays knew that the cost of these essential improvements was too prohibitive for Calgary taxpayers to handle alone. Yet local pride of ownership was a large political obstacle to selling the airfield to the Department of Transport, the only public aviation body that could afford the improvements.

To quiet the environmentalists, Hays persuaded council to rezone the land surrounding the airport as industrial instead of residential. There could at least be no complaints then that the jets kept Calgarians awake at nights, since no one would be living near the airport. The establishment of the McCall Golf Course just south of the airport contributed further to Hays's purpose of keeping the airport where it was.

As for the question of Calgary's jetliner handling capacity compared with Edmonton's, Hays, after some careful checking of Calgary's runway capabilities, decided on an approach that was about two-thirds bluff. He took the position that Calgary's McCall Field was already capable of handling jetliner traffic, especially if the Department of Transport would simply help the city make a few relatively modest expansions to its facilities. In hardly any time at all, he was provided with a fortuitous opportunity to have his case proven—or disproven.

In 1960 Trans-Canada Airlines (later Air Canada) bought Canada's first jetliner, a DC-8. Transport Minister George Hees and officials of his department joined Trans-Canada officials on a cross-country exhibition flight aboard the exciting new flying machine. Hays and other Calgarians, including Arthur Smith and McCall Field manager William Watts, interested in the healthy development of city airport amenities, arranged for Calgary to be one of the jet-liner's landing places, with plenty of fanfare attached to the event. This would prove Hays's claim that McCall Field was already capable of handling jetliners.

What Hays did not publicize was the fact that only one Calgary runway was long enough to handle the fast-flying jetliner, an unsettling enough situation without also considering the relative inexperience of pilots with this newest generation of aircraft. The east-west runway at McCall Field was too short at six thousand feet, and the main north-south runway was barely sufficient at eight thousand feet. It was Hays's understanding that the main runway would have to be used, regardless of wind direction.

The DC-8 flew to Calgary from Vancouver. The plane was not fully loaded with fuel for the short flight, the more readily to brake it to a stop on the short runway. The jetliner not only landed without a hitch; it also took up two groups of Calgarians, Hays among them, on sample flights and landed them safely. For each flight, however, the plane's fuel tanks were only partly filled, both to help ensure that it could get airborne before using up all the available runway, and that it could stop by the end of the runway on landing. Hays recalled how hard the pilot had had to rev the engines for the takeoff, and how hard he had had to press on the brakes for each landing, while the indicator light flashed its warning of too much braking and the tires smoked from the exertion of stopping just short of the end of the runway. But there were no mishaps; the jet-liner managed each takeoff and landing successfully, and Hays made his case.

By the end of his first two-year term as mayor, Hays could point to a $15-million expansion project, including lengthening the run-ways, at McCall Field. He had negotiated this with the federal gov-ernment to accommodate the increasing number of jetliner flights by then calling in at Calgary.

□   □   □

Another element of Napoleon's Paris that caught Hays's attention was its system of wards, each spreading from the city centre and shaped like a slice of pie. Hays liked this scheme because it would ensure that each ward contained a thorough mix of civic challenges for every alderman—a blend of the problems of the poor and the in-terests of the rich, of educational and recreational needs, and of business and commercial demands. The more conventional system of dividing a city into a checkerboard of wards, Hays believed, was bound to create some wards with interests that clashed with in-terests in other wards. This would lead to wasteful clashes among their elected representatives. A Napoleonic ward system for Cal-gary, Hays believed, would reduce, if not remove altogether, the problem of dealing with special interests capable of marshalling greater political influence in support of their causes rather than for policies and programs of greater benefit to the general populace, who are too sprawling and disparate in interests to make them-selves effectively heard except in elections. But Hays was never successful in persuading city council to accept this Napoleonic reform. Today Calgary has a conventional checkerboard system of wards.

As part of his pay-as-you-go civic budget policy, Hays in 1961 had taken a hold-the-line approach both to the pay cheques of civic employees and to city taxes. This led to an extended strike of city transit system drivers beginning in July on the eve of the Stam-pede, when Calgary was jammed with visitors. It was probably the most controversial single position Hays took while he was mayor, even though it had the support of every council member except Morrison. This reflected the fact that Hays's position was more popular with Calgarians than the union's. At one stage the strikers were suspected of being responsible for spraying defoliant on trees at Hays's home, though this was never proven. Worst of all, the strike came during the summer of 1961, the year Hays had to answer for his record in the October civic election. The drivers, then earning $2.09 an hour, stayed on strike for thirty-eight days. But Hays did not budge from his position that there should be no pay increases that year, despite accusations by the Calgary Labour Council that he was a "mouthpiece for millionaires." The drivers finally returned to work with a commitment for a pay increase of nine cents an hour—effective 1 January 1962.

The longer Hays remained in the mayor's office, the more evidence there was of his political acumen. He must have been born with the most important political gift—the one most essential for survival and success in politics: a sensitive intuition for making the right statement, the right move in any crisis. It was an automatic feel for where to step when he unexpectedly found himself walking through a political minefield, and judgement had to be exercised spontaneously, without benefit of a poll. Hays missed all the mines during his first two years in office.

During the summer of 1960, for example, the Calgary Labour Council demanded Hays's resignation for supporting city council's $100,000 cut to the Calgary General Hospital budget. Hays argued that he was acting in the best interests of Labour Council members, and he refused to resign. He told the Labour Council that he had received a mandate from electors "to administer this city on a sound business basis." Close scrutiny had been given to the spending of all city operations. "I have endeavoured to carry out these promises to the best of my ability as I have a great concern for the small taxpayer of the City of Calgary, upon whom taxes fall most heavily. I am convinced that a great number of your membership fall within this group."

Hays had launched an expansion of Calgary's parks system which gave the city during his time in office more park space per capita than any other city of its size in North America. When he announced on 10 June 1961 that he would seek re-election that fall, he said he wanted to finish the work he had begun during his first term. He wanted to see the parks policy through along with the air-port expansion and new hospital development. He pointed out that Calgary had cut its annual capital and operating expenditures by mil-lions of dollars, even though its population had increased by 23,000, nearly 10 per cent. He gave the credit to "a co-operative city coun-cil and an efficient board of administration."

That September, when he launched his second mayoralty cam-paign, Hays took the unusual though characteristic step of saying, "This is the last time I'll ever want to be mayor." He repeated his favourite saying, that there was no room for politics in civic govern-ment, especially party politics, because it was too dependent on the senior levels of government for so much of its revenue.

He offered a subtle political excuse, if not an outright politician's skilled apology, for missing so many social engagements and for in-tending to go on doing so. He saw the job of mayor as "keeping house for 250,000 people—and if you haven't got the beds made and everything dusted, you have no business going out to tea par-ties." But he did not go so far as to promise to reform. On the contrary. "If I'm elected mayor," he declared, "it will be on exactly the same basis."

On the eve of Hays's second mayoralty election on 18 October 1961, the Calgary *Herald* contained a remarkably uncritical apprai-sal of his first term in office. Hays would be surprised if he did not win the election, it read, "but only because of his certainty that he has been doing what Calgary needs. His concern wouldn't be for himself; he has none of the lust for power of the professional office-holder."

The report did conclude that "the jury [was] still out" on Hays's promise of better bus service; but "virtually his only criticism has come from Ald. P. N. R. Morrison. He has veered away from an earlier statement that Mayor Hays has treated council as an equal partner and has complained that council is now under the mayor's thumb. The other 11 aldermen deny this."

One of the first places Hays had visited after becoming mayor was the city jail. He was appalled by the crowded conditions there. He later said he was sure the Humane Society would have gone af-ter any farmer who kept animals in such conditions. Against sub-stantial opposition, he pushed through a plan for construction of both a city police headquarters and jail and a city library in the same civic building, primarily to save costs. Worse in his critics' eyes, he insisted that the building be located in the rundown east end of downtown Calgary.

Alderman Morrison remembered how open to helpful criticism Hays always was. In the original plan, the civic complex was to be built on stilts, to create parking space underneath it. "I pointed out to Hays that he could have that for office space and for the same money build a parking lot right across the street. Within hours he had accepted that notion. That was the kind of person he was." In this, as in all of the other projects he put forward, Hays always had the ready assistance of Batchelor. Charles Lynch reported that Hays had "spearheaded a dramatic new program of civic buildings, including a police headquarters with a penthouse jail regarded as the best in the west. Right now the venerable old city hall is a shambles as construction crews are renovating the interior. Hays puffs away on stogies amid the confusion and preaches the doctrine of cutting costs and increasing efficiency."

In May of Hays's second election year, Morrison delivered a speech that he meant as complimentary advice that Hays should be more of a politician. "Unless Harry Hays pulls up his political socks, we may have another mayor next fall. Harry cares nothing about politics, but he has tried to do a lot for Calgary." Morrison credited Hays with superintending $5.5 million worth of civic construction on a pay-as-you-go basis during the twenty-one months he had so far held office. Financing that amount of construction by debentures, Morrison said, would have cost the city $10 million to $14 million. Morrison did point out that Hays had insisted on a hold-the-line policy with civic wages. But this inflexibility, he said, had earned Hays the enmity of many. "By and large, do citizens care enough about holding the line to swing their votes behind it? I think not."

The Calgary *Herald* responded editorially that "it would certainly be a sad commentary on the people of Calgary" should Morrison be proven right in the coming election. "Somehow, we don't believe [Calgarians] are that shallow. The critics of Mayor Hays have largely been people . . . who have found the mayor unwilling to court popularity by grinding their axes for them. The great majority of

Calgarians may be silent on the question, but they have had a chance to see the man operate, as he promised he would, on a business-like basis."

The editorial even defended Hays against the prospect of a sizable rise in the Calgary tax rate that year. If it came, it would be the result of a Social Credit provincial government educational tax plan—over which, the editorial noted, the mayor had no control. It concluded on a note of incredible political naiveté and misconception of what real political skill is: "Mayor Hays is not a political animal. . . . But . . . if the people of Calgary turn him down because he was not enough of a free-spender and glad-hander, they will get the kind of administration they ask for." As far as the Calgary *Herald* was concerned, Hays had achieved the ultimate in the political art—the rare skill of concealing the art in his art.

Morrison, long afterwards, ruefully recalled the attention attracted by his speech. "This was overcooked. When I made this speech I was trying to praise him. What I was saying was, he was good for the city and bad for his political future. My prediction turned out to be wrong, because the person who ran against him got annihilated in the next election."

By the time Hays had won his second election, he was thoroughly at home in the mayor's office. And he had begun to devote more thought to policies that might make Calgary a better city to live and work in. Unemployment had become a problem in the city, and Hays was casting about for ideas to stimulate the local economy. One policy he developed with some vigour was an ambitious plan to move the Canadian Pacific Railway yards out of downtown Calgary.

The $35-million plan proposed to relocate the CPR yards to the eastern edge of the city. The yards then occupied 102 acres of prime land in the heart of downtown Calgary. They would be moved in return for a single rail line running from east Calgary along the south bank of the Bow River, to connect with the existing tracks where they ran from just west of the city centre and led out of town. This was an enterprising enough proposal in itself, but other aspects of the plan infused it with a futuristic quality that would probably still be exciting today.

Hays saw the plan as a substantial improvement in the overall environment of Calgary. The Bow River running through the city from northwest to southeast was a natural obstacle to the flow of traffic between north and south Calgary. It had to be bridged regardless. Putting artificial obstacles like the railway line and the freeway alongside the river and bridging all three at the same time seemed only reasonable. With attractive landscaping, there need be nothing like an eyesore; on the contrary, both the rail line and the freeway could be designed so as not to interfere with public use of the river bank itself. In return for this arrangement, the railway scar through the centre of downtown Calgary would be permanently removed. The city's downtown core would be united in a single design.

Hays tried to emphasize the potential financial benefits to Calgary taxpayers. A freeway along the river, beside the proposed new railway tracks, would be built, but he expected provincial government help in paying for it. To protect the river bank's parklike qualities, a landscaped buffer strip would border the tracks, concealing them from the river on one side and the freeway on the other. Commercial development of the CPR's 102 acres downtown would yield $90 million in taxes over twenty years. Elimination of the need for more subways under the existing railway tracks would save taxpayers another $6 million over fourteen years.

The plan had been more than three years in the making; negotiations with the CPR had started in December 1959. Interest built up to a feverish pitch during the early months of 1963 and peaked with the formal announcement of the plan's details on Friday, 5 April—just three days before the federal election in which Hays by then was a Liberal candidate against Alderman Jack Leslie, who was running for the Tories. Hays's optimistic confidence that Calgarians would readily accept the plan was manifest when he was asked whether he thought there would be any protest about the freeway and the tracks running along the river bank. "The benefits so outnumber the liabilities," he replied, "that any thinking Calgarian will go along with it."

Ian Sinclair, later chairman of the CPR, commented: "You won't recognize Calgary in twenty years." The Calgary *Herald* editorialized: "Mayor Harry Hays is to be congratulated for the role he played in helping bring this project to Calgary. It is a major accomplishment and will benefit almost every Calgarian far into the future." The Calgary *Albertan* was more cautious in its reaction. The

CPR plan "opens up vistas which the people of this city will need time to get used to," it wrote. "While Calgary may be running few risks, it is confronted by a revolutionary change in the established pattern of traffic and commercial development. . . . Change on so vast a scale is unsettling." Unsettling indeed; the plan quickly became an explosively controversial issue, with environmentalists leading the opposition, and with Hays, soon away to Ottawa, no longer around to defend it as only he could have.

Grant MacEwan supposed from the hindsight of a quarter of a century that the CPR proposal was the most imaginative of all Hays's policy schemes, though MacEwan was among those who finally defeated it. "I don't know whether it was Harry's idea or CP's, but the initial plans were made between CPR people and the mayor, without council. He launched it in Montreal and brought the idea to council after the initial plan had been drawn. I think it was probably done in haste, and council in the long run didn't see fit to endorse it. But still, it certainly was imaginative." Many others, however, disagreed.

As I learned when I worked with Hays while he was minister of agriculture, he liked to move quickly on new policy ideas when any good ones came his way, whether from his own imagination or someone else's. This was the underlying exhilaration of a political job—the opportunity to make what he, at least, thought were improvements in his community. As Hays had quickly learned, the best moment to move on an idea whose time had come, in terms of public support, usually did not last very long. So he moved while he could, confident that even his opponents would see how right he had been once his new policy was in operation.

"Harry wasn't what you'd call an ardent democrat," MacEwan remembered. "He was a man of action. When he thought there was something that should be done, he was going to move to do it."

Hays put forward several other policies, not all of them as grand, or even as serious as his CPR proposal, but which were remarkable at least for their imaginativeness. Early in 1962, while concerns were being expressed about education costs to the taxpayer, Hays worked out how $2 million could be saved: build fewer schools and teach children on a two-shift system. One shift would run from 7 A.M. until noon and the other from 1 P.M. until sometime in the evening.

Alderman Morrison's reaction to this Hays idea inspired the *Herald* headline, "Morrison Claims Mayor Hays Flunks as Education Expert." The story reported Morrison as saying: "Mayor Harry Hays knows nothing about education and he would be 'burned in effigy' if his suggestion for the shift system in Calgary schools were taken seriously." Mothers would have to be up at 5 A.M. to get some of their children ready for the early shift, Morrison scoffed, and they might not see their Grade 1 children home before 7 P.M. The idea was never seriously pursued.

The need to find space for the expansion of the Calgary Exhibition and Stampede grounds, in the Victoria Park area on the southeastern edge of downtown, inspired another unique solution from Hays: rechannel the Elbow River from its course around the southeast perimeter of the grounds to a route along the northwest perimeter. Then the grounds could be extended farther southeast into unpeopled, reclaimed industrial land. This idea did not fly, either, except as a brief news novelty. The Stampede grounds gradually took over more and more of the residential area in Victoria Park, a source of extended controversy in Calgary civic politics long after Hays had left the mayor's office.

Hays had by now achieved enough political stature in Calgary to have caught the attention of three political parties—the Social Credit, whose provincial government, then under Premier E. C. Manning, had dominated Alberta since 1935; the Progressive Conservatives, at that time long out of power in Alberta but willing to offer Hays substantial financial guarantees to becomes its provincial party leader; and the Liberals, under Lester Pearson, at that time leader of the Opposition against the Diefenbaker government. The lure of action in a larger political arena was to prove more than Hays could resist.

Without his leadership, Calgary city council gradually frittered away the redevelopment opportunities Hays had created in the rail removal plan. Hays once confided that the CPR executives had decided weeks before the final council vote that they wanted to back out of the plan. He said he had been informed privately that the railway had lost confidence in the capacity of the elected city administration to carry through such an enormous project. Its executives laid down such tough conditions for going ahead with the project that council was virtually forced to reject it. That way, the railway achieved what it wanted, but any blame for rejecting the plan was directed at city council.

On 22 June 1964, after some two years of bitter, partisan and, in Hays's view, short-sighted bickering over the plan led by Alderman Jack Leslie, Calgary city council, led by Hays's successor, Mayor Grant MacEwan, voted ten to three to kill the plan, primarily because of the environmentalists' opposition to having the railway and freeway along the river bank.

The railway scar across downtown Calgary remains to this day. Memorial Drive on the north bank of the Bow has been expanded into a four-lane crosstown parkway. And two lines of Calgary's Light Rail Transit system run between the parkway lanes for part of its stretch along the river.

CHAPTER EIGHT

AN
ALBERTA
LIBERAL

Not everyone who knew Harry Hays loved or admired or even respected him. He had his share of critics, as anyone active in politics is bound to have. Some regarded him as an absolute opportunist. They claimed that he jumped in for self-ambition, for self-glorification, with opportune timing. There was admittedly a void in the Calgary mayoralty at the time Hays made his initial election bid, but it was undeniably courageous of the relatively unknown and untrained Hays to run for that post. Nevertheless, there were still people who looked at the history of his accessions and were convinced that each occasion indicated a leap-frog caused by his ambition more than by anything else.

Similiar criticism was directed against Hays for his move into federal politics in 1963. Hays had faced a tight race against Don

Mackay on his first run for the mayor's office. Clearly the first civic election was by no means an obvious opportunity, but a gamble for Hays. He won his second mayoralty campaign with a landslide of votes, earned by his own record in office. And if his first civic run was a gamble, certainly leaping into federal politics as that rarest of political species, an Alberta Liberal, was an even longer one.

In the federal election of June 1962, the mighty political colossus that John Diefenbaker had fashioned for the Progressive Conservatives with his 208-seat win in 1958 was cut to a minority of 116 of the 265 House of Commons seats. But none of the 99 seats the Pearson Liberals won in 1962 were held in Alberta. And when Hays decided to run as a Liberal in the 1963 election, he chose, mainly because he had lived there for years, the riding of Calgary South, which had elected only one Liberal in its entire history: M. J. Edwards had won it by a mere 403 votes in the wartime election of 1940, when a lot of people would have considered it unpatriotic not to vote for the sitting government of the day, the Liberals.

Furthermore, Calgary South had been the riding of former Conservative prime minister R. B. Bennett from 1925 until 1940. Arthur Smith's late father, A. L. Smith, won the seat back for the Conservatives in 1945—and even in the 1962 election, so disastrous for his fellow Tories, Arthur Smith won the seat, for his third time in a row, by nine thousand votes. Even though Smith dropped out of federal politics after the February 1963 defeat of the Diefenbaker government precipitated an election for 8 April, Hays had no assurance that he would be a winning Liberal candidate in Calgary South.

"I never did feel that he was a Liberal in the sense of a liberal traditionalist," Arthur Smith recalled. "He made it abundantly clear to everyone that he was a Liberal by persuasion. He wasn't quite sure what the philosophical differences were between being a Liberal and a Conservative." Hays himself stated: "The Liberals are in office and the Conservatives aren't—that's the main difference." There is a story of a friend of his who said: "Harry, you're going to make me do something I've never done in my life—vote Liberal." Replied Hays: "Don't let it worry you. I've never voted Liberal in my life, either."

As surprised as anyone that Hays ran for federal office under any political banner, especially the Liberal, was his son, Dan, since 1984 a senator.

> We argued a lot about politics. I remember voting for the first time. He didn't tell me who he voted for, and I don't know why he didn't tell me. I suspect he voted Social Credit.
>
> I was active in Liberal politics before he was. I went to the University of Alberta in 1958. I lived in residence, and there were a number of friends—Jim Coutts was a couple of years ahead of me. We became involved in political activity at university.
>
> My father and I would have arguments about my support of the Liberal party. I don't think he had a high opinion of politicians before he went into politics himself. Except for some individuals. He had a tremendous regard for Ernest Manning at that time. That may have changed over the years. I think they were always friends, but I think after his own experience in politics, he saw all politicians in a different light. I'd have thought he wouldn't have been fair then in his assessment of the Liberal politicians of that time.

Rumours that Hays might run as a Liberal had begun to appear in the Calgary news media early in February 1963. The Calgary *Herald* reported that Hays had denied any political ambitions. Apparently he did not want to leave his Calgary business for the long months while Parliament was in session. This was two weeks before his announcement that he was running. The Calgary *Albertan* called it the worst-kept secret of the campaign just a couple of days before Hays made a formal announcement to a special meeting of Calgary city council on 19 February. The closed-doors council meeting voted unanimously that Hays should stay on as mayor at least until the election results were in. "I'll go see them again the day after the election," Hays told reporters, "and see what they want me to do."

Alderman Jack Leslie, destined to run as the Conservative candidate against Hays, said the mayor's decision came as no surprise. "It doesn't change any of my plans. I'll just have to work harder."

What finally tilted Hays into his decision, he often said afterward, was his respect for Lester Pearson. But Keith Davey, then the young, energetic national organizer of the Liberal party, made the bold initial pitch that lured Hays into becoming an Alberta Liberal. And Walter Gordon, chairman of the party's National Campaign Committee, played an important role, as did Jim Coutts as the Liberal campaign chairman in Alberta.

Keith Davey first met Hays in the fall of 1962. Jim Coutts, after losing that year's election in Macleod (a campaign managed by Hays's son, Dan), had decided he would not run again, at least not for a while, and accepted Davey's invitation to become the party's Alberta campaign chairman. In the fall of 1962 Davey met with a group of Alberta Liberals in Calgary, including Coutts and long-time Calgary Liberal grassroots worker J. Cameron Millikin. He told them:

> "Look, forget the party labels. We want the guy who can win a seat here."
> And they said, "There's no question—it's Harry Hays." So I said, "Okay, let's go and see him." They said, "The guy's the mayor. We don't know if he's a Liberal or what he is." That's how I met him. I just went to his city hall office on a cold call. Harry was interested. The idea just appealed to him.

Nevertheless, Hays flew down to Ottawa and met with Pearson, who very possibly promised him a cabinet post if he ran and won.

Hays, while interested, was not so easily persuaded. As he later revealed, he even turned down Pearson the first time they discussed the idea. And he raised some specific obstacles with Davey during their initial Calgary city hall meeting. Davey thought the best way to deal with these reservations was to let Hays talk directly to campaign committee chairman Walter Gordon by telephone right then. Gordon remembered:

> The first time I ever heard of Harry Hays was in a call from Keith Davey in Calgary saying that he was with Hays, who was the mayor, and he thought he could win Calgary South. But he was unhappy about the Liberal party's agricultural policy, so would I speak to him? Harry came on the line and said, "I'd like to run, but I don't see how I could as a Liberal when I disagree with the party's agriculture policy." I said, "Well, I disagree with it, too. Why don't you run and change it?" He said, "Are you serious?" And I said, "Sure. It's not

much of a policy. We haven't got anybody around who knows much about agriculture. If you're interested, why don't you get yourself elected and then change it around." So he said, "All right." And that was that.

But not quite. Davey still had the delicate task of tactfully dissuading the losing Calgary South Liberal candidate in the 1962 election to stand aside for Hays. He was Rev. Frank Morley, then the very popular minister at the city's downtown Grace Presbyterian Church, whose congregation included Calgary Establishment members such as millionaire oilman and racehorse-breeder Max Bell, who was supporting Morley's candidacy. Davey remembered how difficult his breakfast meeting with Morley and his wife to broach this matter had been. He succeeded in his objective, but this done, there was still the challenge of getting Hays elected. It did not look easy.

Just before Hays flew to Ottawa to meet Pearson, Davey received the results of a survey in Calgary South, and they were not promising. At the Calgary airport Hays asked Coutts if he had had any word on the survey; Coutts assured him the results looked fine and said they would talk about it when Hays got back.

Having returned to Calgary, Hays made no public mention of his meeting with Pearson. He only said that he had had further discussions about the idea of running federally with Mitchell Sharp, the former deputy minister of trade who had resigned, in part out of sheer outrage at Diefenbaker, to run successfully as a Liberal in Toronto in 1962.

Hays told city hall reporters that he had decided to run after having lunch with Sharp in Ottawa. "His sacrifices are probably greater than mine," Hays said. "And he pointed out that it's a challenge." Perhaps most significant, Sharp was firmly of the opinion that the Liberals would form the next government. Hays had never cared to be part of a losing team; Sharp convinced him he would have to run as a Liberal if he wanted to be with the winners— though Hays had no illusions about how large his personal political challenge was going to be in Calgary South.

Hays explained his decision simply: "I was impressed with Mr. Pearson and his policies. He's got hardboiled proposals to cure some economic ills, including unemployment."

(Later that autumn Hays was more forthcoming about Pearson's influence on his decision. The chamber of commerce in his home town of Carstairs, under the presidency of Hays's old friend Curtis Clark, arranged a dinner in his honour. In his speech, Hays said: "In my tour of eight countries of Europe, I had people in high places who I didn't know come up and tell me Pearson was the greatest Canadian, and that without him, the world would now have been fighting the Third World War.")

The news media attached great importance to knowing whether or not the promise of a cabinet post had been made. If Hays did win, he was likely to be the only Liberal elected in Alberta. Promise or no promise, then, he would be virtually assured of a cabinet position. The big challenge, however, was not getting a cabinet job but winning the Calgary South seat.

Instead of worrying, Hays adopted a genial take-it-or-leave-it approach to campaigning. In a few interviews on radio and television, he said, in effect, that he was making himself available to serve the voters of Calgary South in Parliament to the best of his ability; if they wanted him there, they could vote for him, and if they did not want him, they could vote for someone else, and he would not take it personally. He would still find plenty to do in the mayor's office, though about a year previous he had reconfirmed his decision not to run for a third term, no matter what: "I don't want this job any more," he told city hall reporters in March 1962. "I have enjoyed it, but I know when I have had enough."

Hays's unique approach to running for federal office, an approach almost defying Calgarians in his mostly well-to-do riding to vote for him if they wanted what would be best for them, caught the attention of roaming reporter Charles Lynch. As recently as 1963, a political candidate's religion could still be an issue. Lynch noted that the religious situation within the Hays family might be a political handicap in other provinces, but apparently not in Alberta. Hays explained to Lynch that he was Roman Catholic, his wife was Anglican, and their son, Dan, brought up an Anglican, had married a Catholic and decided their children should be raised Catholic; furthermore, his seven brothers and sisters, all Catholics, had all married Protestants.

"Mother always said there would be no trouble if the children were brought up in the faith of the mother, and she was right.

We're a happy family, and there have been no divorces. We have Anglicans, United Church, Mormons and some in the family of a new religion I can't name. I have lived with a Protestant for twenty-seven years, and it's wonderful."

Lynch referred to Hays's unbounded admiration for Alberta Premier E. C. Manning, quoting Hays as calling him "a terrific man"—an opinion that would eventually have sharp irony in it. Lynch wrote in the Calgary *Herald* that Hays thought Pearson might be as good a prime minister as Manning was a premier. "Manning runs this province on a businesslike basis," Hays said; "Pearson convinced me that he plans to conduct a good, solid business government."

Lynch also reported what for Hays was a strictly followed policy for the first couple of years of his federal political career—that no one associated with his campaign should ever publicly say anything critical of John Diefenbaker, even though he was still leader of the opposing political forces the Liberals had to beat. "Hays, who looks like E. P. Taylor and talks like C. D. Howe, has nothing bad to say about Prime Minister Diefenbaker," Lynch wrote, "except that 'he doesn't reach me.' Visiting Liberal speakers who are flocking in to help him are told to lay off the rough stuff on Diefenbaker."

Hays's reasoning behind this policy was another indication of the astuteness of his own political instincts. When I joined his staff about a year later, he explained to me that there was no sense in criticizing Diefenbaker in an area where everyone had been voting for him for years. Maybe they had begun to change their minds, but Hays believed open criticism of the Tory chief would only get voters' backs up by forcing them to face the unwelcome fact that they may have been wrong. "You don't win their support by rubbing their faces in their own mistakes," he said.

The Hays organization set up campaign headquarters in a basement at 1011 17th Avenue S.W. Since he was running in Smith's old seat, Hays could expect no help from his Tory friend in this campaign, even though Smith's intimates knew that by now he had come to despise Diefenbaker. Six sitting aldermen, including Grant MacEwan and P. N. R. Morrison, worked on his campaign, along with two former aldermen, including Don McIntosh. A red-haired bread truck driver with a volatile temper, McIntosh had been a supporter of the NDP when Hays first became mayor and one of his most ready critics. But Hays had treated McIntosh so fairly and had handled city affairs so much to his liking that by then he was an adoring fan.

Calgary oil millionaire Carl Nickle was the Conservative M.P. for Calgary South prior to Art Smith. With Morrison, a former supporter of the CCF, he set up a citizens' committee to support Hays, in part because of his dislike of Diefenbaker's approach to government.

Hays continued to act as mayor while conducting his federal election campaign. He was not by nature a door-knocking campaigner, though he had plenty of workers who door-knocked on his behalf. He was not much for coffee parties, either; he only attended six during the whole campaign.

Even though Hays and other Liberals managed to attract a crowd of nearly two thousand to Pearson's luncheon speech in the Palliser Hotel, all indications were that the election was going to be extremely close. No one was encouraged when Hays fell ill with flu for three days during the week before the election. And the early returns on election night kept the atmosphere in the basement headquarters tense. The lead seesawed between Hays and his Tory opponent, Alderman Jack Leslie.

Hays arrived at the headquarters at about 7:30 on election night. Outwardly he was the least concerned person in the room. He looked at the early returns and remarked on the obvious: "It's pretty close." The results flowing in by telephone, radio and television continued to seesaw. "What's the use of getting worried?" Hays murmured. But he was soon huddled over a transistor radio, listening for the latest results. Then the trend began to swing his way a little more. He was ahead by a thousand votes. "That's a little better," he said and began to relax.

Someone congratulated him on the birth of his first grandchild, Carol, to his son's wife, Linda, in Toronto, where Dan was then studying law. He responded with enthusiasm: "I was nine feet tall when I heard that. I just spit right across the road."

Finally, with only a few polls still to be heard from, word reached the Hays headquarters that Alderman Leslie was on his way over to concede defeat. "There it goes," Hays said, shaking hands with his jubilant supporters and grinning widely. Quipping his way through the crowd, he laughed: "I hope I've exploded the theory that coffee parties win elections. They're not only tough on the stomach but hard on the feet." To another well-wisher he grinned: "I feel just like a young colt."

When asked how he explained his taking the riding for the Liberals after twenty-three years of unbroken Tory domination, Hays had a one-word answer: "Diefenbaker."

As it turned out, however, Diefenbaker still held sway in western Canada. Hays was the only Liberal elected in Alberta and Saskatchewan. The final results in Calgary South showed just how close his victory had been: he received 21,030 votes—or 39.50 per cent—to Leslie's 19,693—or 36.90 per cent, a spread of only 1337 votes. Across the country, the Pearson Liberals had won the election, though with a minority of seats in the Commons, 128 to the Conservatives' 96. But it was enough to put Pearson into the prime minister's office—and Harry Hays into the office of minister of agriculture.

He would quickly discover that it was a far different place from the mayor's office.

CHAPTER NINE

LEARNING TO MINISTER

By the time he was sworn in as minister of agriculture on 22 April 1963, Harry Hays had a crowded platter of responsibilities facing him. He was also almost immediately plunged into political hot water.

The most urgent cabinet demand on him was to prepare, get cabinet approval for and be ready to announce—in only eight days—a new national dairy policy for the twelvemonth beginning 1 May. He was still the mayor of Calgary, and he knew that within weeks he was to be named governor of the vast Rotary International District 536, an honour he was reluctant to decline, but one which he knew would make onerous demands on his time. And there was Hays's growing awareness that Ottawa's Parliament Hill was a political minefield of substantially greater complexity and sophistication than Calgary's City Hall.

Nor had Prime Minister Pearson, in the design of his new cabinet, done much to enhance Hays's stature in his critics' eyes. Pearson named Mitchell Sharp minister of trade and transferred to him cabinet responsibility for the Canadian Wheat Board, which had been under the jurisdiction of the ministry of agriculture. An added complication for Hays was a Liberal campaign promise, aimed at pleasing farmers in eastern Canada, to create for the first time the post of associate minister of agriculture to help look after their interests. As far as Hays was concerned, the possibilities for internal cabinet conflict were almost infinite in such a setup. Traditionally, the agriculture minister had been from western Canada. Quebecker René Tremblay was slated for this new post once it could be legislated into existence. (It never was, because Hays convinced his cabinet colleagues that agriculture policies had to be implemented on a national, not a regional, basis.) Meanwhile Tremblay was appointed minister without portfolio.

Developing a new dairy program in eight days was a pressing challenge for Hays from the moment he arrived at Department of Agriculture headquarters, just across the street from Parliament Hill in the Confederation Building. The underlying problem was a subsidy program, for which Alvin Hamilton, Diefenbaker's minister of agriculture, had been responsible. The program did not recognize the practical division of the dairy industry into two sectors with quite different policy needs—the drinking-milk sector and the manufacturing-milk sector. It had produced an enormous surplus of unsalable butter, was costing about $40 million a year, and showed no signs of doing better.

Hays's long experience as a dairyman, coupled with his department's suggestion that there was a better chance of selling cheese than butter at that time, led him to swiftly begin shifting the subsidy towards a more workable direction, though few of the reporters who would soon be writing such critical and amusing stories about him discerned this.

On 1 May Hays announced changes in the subsidy program intended both to encourage more production of cheese and less of butter in the manufacturing sector and to discourage drinking-milk producers from producing a surplus which they dumped into the manufacturing sector to take advantage of government subsidy payments. He did this by raising the subsidy for milk used in cheese production by five cents per hundred pounds, providing for government purchase of certain amounts of skim milk, and by removing a twenty-five-cent federal government payment to producers for drinking milk.

Country Guide, typifying initial reaction, editorialized: "A gesture has been made to shift milk from butter to cheese production. . . . [But] these measures, which Mr. Hays said were intended to bring production and consumption into better balance, are unlikely to be effective."

Hays would probably have agreed that his dairy policy left something to be desired, but not that his measures would have no effect. Nor, though he did so with some caution, did he hesitate to defend himself on this and other issues right from the start of his new career. Again, this seemed to go unnoticed by his press gallery critics.

In the Commons on the first working day of the new Parliament, 16 May 1963, Hays argued of his dairy program that "we had only two or three days to take care of this policy. This matter should have been taken care of long ago." He defended his position further that fall by attacking the policy of the Diefenbaker government: "In 1958 the previous government raised the price of butter from fifty-eight cents to sixty-four cents per pound, and now we are subsidizing it at both ends, twelve cents per pound to the consumer and a great deal to the producer. We cannot live with that sort of thing, and we must think of some different way to help the dairy farmer."

By December Hays could offer evidence that his initial dairy policy was having a noticeable effect. In the Commons he quoted a statement made by J. M. Hartwick, president of the National Dairy Council of Canada, about his subsidy changes: "A shift to cheese production from butter has helped provide the dairy industry with the most optimistic situation experienced in many years. It is now almost certain that cheddar cheese sales in Canada this year will record an all-time high of well over 105 million pounds."

Yet this and other policy successes Hays might be achieving were dramatically overshadowed virtually from the day Parliament opened by a rather astonishing variety of controversies swirling around him, none of which had much, if anything, to do with agriculture.

The first controversy developed over Hays's decision, with city council's approval, to remain as mayor of Calgary after his appointment to cabinet. The main reason for this was Hays's key role in negotiating the deal with the CPR—and explaining and selling it to Calgary voters—to relocate the railways' downtown yards and main line. In the hope of getting the deal through, Hays agreed to stay on as mayor in absentia, so to speak, at a salary of $1 a year. Each councillor took a turn at being deputy mayor for one month at a time until a new mayor could be elected that October. For Hays it meant working as minister of agriculture in Ottawa through the week, then flying to Calgary to work as mayor during the weekend.

The strongest criticism of this arrangement came from Calgary labour leaders. Leo Chikinda, president of the fifteen-thousand-member Calgary Labour Council, demanded that Hays resign from the mayor's job immediately. "The city requires a full-time mayor," he said. Even more critical was John Hannigan, business agent for the Sheet Metal Workers' Union. "He should have resigned his post the minute he became an M.P. A man can only hold down one job at a time and do it well. I think it is reducing local government to a farce. Mayor Hays is lowering the dignity of the office." But Harley Horne, business agent for the two-thousand-member Civic Employees' Union, though not in favour of the idea of an absent mayor, said that "things seem to be rolling along without him."

Hays ignored the criticism and tried to make the arrangement work. But after only a few weeks, he heeded the advice of his new friend in cabinet, Finance Minister Walter Gordon. On 17 June he submitted to the Calgary council his resignation as mayor, effective 30 June, stating that the position conflicted with his duties as minister of agriculture. This did not, however, produce much of an improvement in his schedule of duties, for a few days later, at a convention in St. Louis, Missouri, he was elected governor of District 536 of Rotary International, effective 1 July—one day after he stepped down as mayor. His governor duties included visiting and speaking to every one of the thirty-six individual Rotary clubs in the district—twenty-nine in Alberta, five in Saskatchewan and two in British Columbia—during the next year.

The demands made on his time by the mayor's job had already contributed to the second controversy, concerning Hays's absences from the Commons, though another, unpublicized, reason for his absences was his early conviction that the daily Question Period, during which most of the criticism was levelled, was a total waste of time. This controversy was fed by a third criticism that arose over his continued activities as an auctioneer. In most cases he was completing contractual commitments made before his election to Parliament, and he had stopped accepting any payment from the time he entered cabinet. One of the first to suggest that auctioneering was improper for an agriculture minister was former prime minister Diefenbaker.

Parliament had been in session barely ten days when Diefenbaker, scowling at his imperious best, rose in the Commons and directed this question at Prime Minister Pearson, in Hays's absence: "Does the prime minister consider it appropriate for a minister of the crown in charge of the portfolio of agriculture to be engaged in the auctioneering of cattle at an auction sale, and is not such a course in his view not in keeping, as I believe it is not, with the proprieties that one expects?"

The Opposition leader gave no indication of when or where Hays had been acting as an auctioneer since becoming a cabinet minister—perhaps because his keen political instincts sensed Hays's auction clients might resent any suggestion that helping them get a good price for their animals was improper, especially for their own minister of agriculture. The political fallout might land on the critic in this case, instead of on the criticized. At any rate, Pearson responded that he would discuss the matter with Hays and reply to Diefenbaker the next day. However, he did not reply the next day, nor did Diefenbaker bring it up.

But Jack Horner, an Alberta Tory M.P., did bring it up the next day. "I notice that he [Hays] is not in his seat," he said; "Perhaps he is still auctioning cattle." Nova Scotia Tory Robert C. Coates incurred Pearson's displeasure by chiming in: "When can we expect the minister of agriculture to resume his duties in the House of Commons?" Pearson responded: "That's obviously an improper question. The minister of agriculture is a very hard-working minister, and he is doing his job."

These criticisms combined were having an unfavourable impact on Hays's public image, especially among some reporters in the Parliamentary Press Gallery. Alvin Hamilton had been something of a news media favourite while a minister in the Diefenbaker government. His relations with high-powered journalists like Peter Newman had been enhanced by the accessibility of his feverishly energetic special assistant, Roy Faibish, the frequent unidentified "reliable source" behind their inside stories about Diefenbaker government dilemmas. Faibish, remembered by upper-echelon agriculture department officials as a sharp-tongued terror to work with, had done much to promote Hamilton's large and positive public reputation.

Not all of Faibish's publicity gambits were wholly legitimate, however, as Newman revealed in his best-selling book about the Diefenbaker years, *Renegade In Power*. One of Hamilton's biggest single claims to success as minister of agriculture was that he had personally sold a lot of Canadian wheat to the Communist Chinese, a claim Faibish tried tirelessly to exploit. But as Hays had learned from his departmental officials when he took over Hamilton's office in April, and as Newman reported that fall, this was simply not so. The contract had been signed between the Canadian Wheat Board and the China State Resources Company three days before Hamilton flew to Hong Kong ostensibly to negotiate the deal. This Hong Kong trip had been Faibish's idea.

To Hays, such inside knowledge made criticism directed at him by Newman all the more galling. "Even to the Liberals, the man who turned out to be the biggest disappointment of the first sixty days in office was Harry Hayes [*sic*]," Newman wrote in *Maclean's* magazine. "In a cabinet whose ministers seem remarkably engrossed in their departmental affairs, Hayes stands out as a man who has given official Ottawa at least the impression of not being too concerned about running his portfolio."

Newman did concede that Hays had a hard image-act to follow.

No other minister came into his job with so many strikes against him. Hayes' predecessor, Alvin Hamilton, was probably the most popular minister of agriculture in Canadian history. He had worked as a farmer. He is a true prairie radical and an able parliamentarian. But Hayes, on the other hand, is not a farmer, and is something of a reactionary. He has failed to show up well in the Commons, though this is hardly surprising in a House where eight of every ten opposition desks are occupied by men from rural ridings.

Newman was wrong on two counts: Hamilton, by his own admission, had never been a farmer, only a farm hand, and Hays had been and still was a farmer.

An examination of the Hansard Commons debates during the early months of Hays's initiation suggests that he was being cautious until he could learn some of the ropes in his new political environment. To an early question from NDP leader T. C. ("Tommy") Douglas as to when the government would be introducing the two-price policy for wheat promised by defeated Saskatchewan Liberal candidate Hazen Argue (a former New Democrat who'd lost that party's leadership race to Douglas), Hays replied with the oldest ministerial put-off in the book: "We should like to take the question as notice." He never did come back with an answer; nor did he ever introduce the two-price wheat policy, which he opposed as unworkable. Argue, meanwhile, went unprotesting to the Senate.

Hays displayed a little more boldness when replying to a question from Lawrence Kindt, the Tory from Alberta who had beaten Jim Coutts in 1962. "We are going to take a look at all agricultural policies as one relates to the other," he said, describing what he had already started doing.

But initially, Hays did not respond publicly to his critics. As he later explained, he had decided to do in the office of minister of agagriculture the same thing that he had done when he first arrived in the Calgary mayor's office. He wanted to give some careful forethought to the kind of policies his new job called for before taking initiatives, so that he would not go off half-cocked into the federal political minefields.

Hays met with each of the provincial agriculture ministers to hear what ideas they had. He also made a nineteen-day visit to Britain, France, Russia, Denmark, Holland and Finland to seek ideas from their ministers of agriculture. As he had done as mayor when he travelled on Calgary business, he took along a couple of his top bureaucrats, Deputy Minister S. C. Barry and Agricultural Stabilization Board Chairman S. B. ("Syd") Williams, to ensure that they would be aware of and supportive of any policies that came of the trip.

Walter Gordon admired the unsung skill with which Hays spearheaded a large sale of Canadian wheat during that visit to the Soviet

The Hays family, Carstairs, 1937. Seated: Dr. Thomas
E. and Sarah. Standing, left to right: Jack, Audrey,
Catherine, Tom, Virginia, Laura, Jean and Harry.
Courtesy Laura Shaw.

Harry, aged twelve, riding his first purchase, which cost him $25. Neighbour Martin Youseph remembers Harry, aged four, his legs barely long enough to straddle his horse, riding bareback to Youseph's farm to ask him to come to the Hays farm to help stamp down silage. "If you can't come over and help," said Hays most seriously, "then I guess I'll have to do it myself." *Courtesy Muriel Hays.*

Catherine, Harry and Tom at the spurious grave of Mickey, the family dog, in 1925. The bereaved girls had wanted a proper burial, though unknown to them, the boys had already tossed the dead dog into the manure pile. *Courtesy Laura Shaw.*

LEFT: Loading the first shipment of Canadian cattle bound for Cuba, 1946. *Courtesy Muriel Hays.*

BELOW: Hays's official portrait when he was fieldman for the Dominion Holstein-Friesian Association, 1933–34. *Courtesy Muriel Hays.*

BOTTOM LEFT: Harry's birthplace, the original Hays dairy farm at Carstairs, showing the three-level barn built in 1911. *Courtesy Laura Shaw.*

Muriel, Dan and Harry, Calgary, 1947. *Courtesy Muriel Hays.*

Muriel and Harry Hays embrace at their silver wedding anniversary celebration in 1959, at the Old Timers' Memorial Building, Calgary. *Courtesy Calgary* Herald.

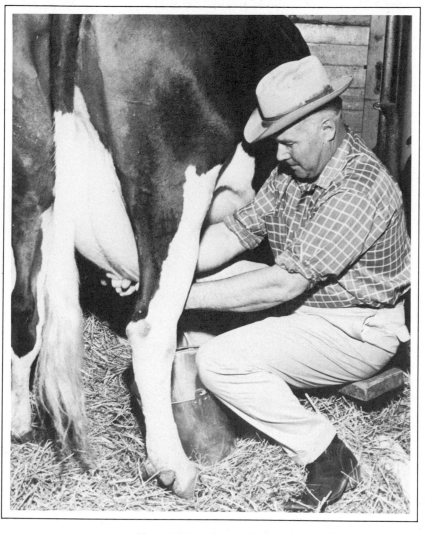

Hays milking Alcartra Gerben, holder of the world record for butterfat production from 1945 to 1954. If all the publicity that Alcartra Gerben obtained following her record had been given a cash value at prevailing advertising rates, the total would have exceeded a million dollars. *Courtesy Muriel Hays.*

Incumbent mayor Don
Mackay congratulates
Hays on his winning the
Calgary mayoralty
election, 14 October
1959. *Courtesy Calgary*
Herald.

Opposition Leader
Lester B. Pearson with
Hays and a constituent
during a 1963 campaign
luncheon at Calgary's
Palliser Hotel. *Courtesy
Calgary* Herald.

Hays auctioning Angus cattle at the 1962 National Jubilee Aberdeen Angus Show at the Calgary Exhibition grounds. *Courtesy Muriel Hays.*

Hays follows vote calculations closely on election night, 9 April 1963. He won the federal Calgary South seat for the Liberals. *Courtesy Calgary* Herald.

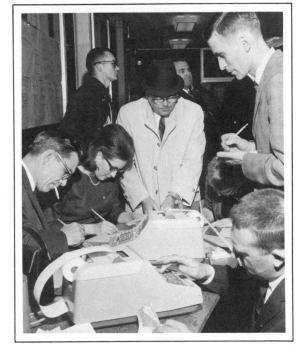

Partners Jenkins and Hill join Hays in mixing sillabub during the 1964 Stampede breakfast. *Courtesy Calgary Herald.*

Prime Minister Pearson, Maryon Pearson and Muriel Hays at the Hays Stampede breakfast, July 1964. *Courtesy Calgary* Herald.

ABOVE: Hays with Soviet Agriculture Minister Ivan P. Volovchenko on a prairie farm in August 1964. Hays had visited the Soviet Union the year before. *Courtesy Canapress Photo Service.*

TOP RIGHT: Senator Hays judging cattle at the National Livestock Show in Nairobi, Kenya. *Courtesy Muriel Hays.*

BOTTOM RIGHT: Hays holding the first pure French Charolais sold at auction in North America; Amour de Paris fetched a price of $58,000 in Calgary. As agriculture minister in 1965, Hays changed animal health regulations that had prevented the importation of Charolais. *Courtesy Muriel Hays.*

Hays auctioneering at his Alberta ranch, November 1963. *Courtesy Calgary* Herald.

Hays confers with brother Tom (l) during cattle auction at the Hays ranch, November 1963. *Courtesy Calgary* Herald.

Hays milking a cow for sillabub ingredients at the
twenty-eighth Stampede breakfast in 1979. *Courtesy
Canapress Photo Service.*

Hays and M.P. Serge Joyal chairing a hearing of the joint Senate-Commons Constitution committee. Two of Hays's sisters were bitterly cruel of his support of Pierre Trudeau's plan to patriate the Constitution. *Courtesy Canapress Photo Service.*

Union—a sale that contributed significantly to record-breaking wheat exports that crop year, 1963–64.

Hays drove to Moscow from a point outside, and he did what he always did when he was going through farmland—he would stop every so many miles and walk into the fields. Doing this on the way to Moscow, he soon realized that the harvest was a disaster. There had been a lot of rain, and the wheat was mouldy. According to Gordon, when Hays arrived in Moscow he went to see the minister of agriculture, Ivan P. Volovchenko, and he said, "Well, I've just come in to commiserate with you on this disaster."

The minister did not know what Hays was talking about. Hays explained that he had seen the condition of the crops, had realized it was a disaster, and then offered Canada's help. Volovchenko asked Hays to return the next day. In the meantime he did some quick research, and he found that Hays was right.

Canada at that time had a vast surplus of wheat that the government did not know how to dispose of; it was being stored wherever it could be stored, including out in the fields, on the ground. Hays told the minister that Canada would be glad to sell the Soviets some wheat, and the minister more or less made a deal with him right away. But he told Hays that he would have to send a committee to Canada to go through the motions of negotiation, and there would have to be a mild concession on the price to make it acceptable for political purposes. Hays said he needed to discuss that with his cabinet colleagues in Ottawa.

Gordon recalled what happened when Hays reached Copenhagen on his way home from Russia.

He called me about the wheat sale and said we'd have to make a mild concession on the price. He didn't want to imply to the Russians that we could do this if I thought he couldn't get it through cabinet. I said, "Of course I will support you a hundred per cent in getting it through cabinet, and I think you can assume that if you and I are for this deal, it will go through." So he then telephoned the Russian minister and said, "Send your committee out; I'm sure we can meet your requirements."

Which was what was done. I thought it was a marvellous deal and I thought he'd handled it beautifully. He knew what he was doing.

The Russian wheat sale enabled Hays to report the following to the annual Federal-Provincial Agricultural Outlook Conference in Ottawa on 23 November 1964:

> The 1963–64 crop year, which ended last July 31, was the most successful wheat marketing year in our nation's history. Production in 1963 reached 723 million bushels, a level never before attained by Canada. Export shipments of wheat and flour totalled an unprecedented 594 million bushels. The previous record high mark of 408 million bushels had been unchallenged since 1928–29.

□   □   □

In December 1963, while in Calgary promoting *Renegade In Power,* Newman took another shot at Hays that received wide coverage from his home-town news media. Newman said Hays was "incredibly inept" and described him as "a rancher who doesn't understand the problems of farmers." By then Hays had begun to fire back at his critics.

He made his first speech in the Commons on 14 October 1963, when his departmental spending estimates came up for approval. The House listened to Alvin Hamilton's lengthy speech on agricultural matters, laden with farm income figures that Hays considered dubious at best and attempting to lay blame on the new Liberal agriculture minister. As Hamilton was finishing his speech, Walter Gordon rushed to Hays's place in the Commons to remind him that he did not need to respond immediately. But the angry Hays was already on his feet to catch the eye of the Speaker. Hays said: "Believe me, I think he is just talking a lot of junk."

The vehemence of his attack on Hamilton startled some fellow Liberals as well as Hamilton's colleagues and seemed, momentarily at least, to bewilder Hamilton himself. Some of the anger behind the attack had been building up for several months. Hays had quickly come to the conclusion that Hamilton had been greatly overrated as an agriculture minister, and that most of his reputation rested on clever public relations activities rather than imaginative farm policies. He also had seen a clipping from the Calgary *Albertan* of an interview with Hamilton during the early weeks of Hays's federal career. It had been a stinger.

The headline read: "Hamilton Not Wild About Harry; Ex-Minister Contends Hays Doesn't Know Job." The story proceeded to quote Hamilton as saying, "Hays isn't really trying. . . . How can Hays hope to learn his department—even the little bit that's left—when he's going off to Rotary conventions?"

We asked him a lot of questions at first, but after a couple of days, I told the boys to lay off and give him a chance to learn his job. Then he jumped right in the soup by going off to Oakville to auctioneer, then he went to the mayors' convention and the Rotary meeting. I asked him when he came back for an answer to my question. He had forgotten what it was. I told him where he could find it in Hansard. He picked up a book on voting records and started leafing through it. He didn't even know what Hansard looked like.

According to Hamilton, Hays once told the Commons that he would answer questions " 'when this wild session of Parliament is over.' This is the quietest it's been [in the Commons] in seven years. He doesn't know what it's all about."

Hays began his attack:

I have travelled in something like thirty-two different countries in the world, and I feel that I know a little bit about agriculture. Until three years ago, I owned and supervised a farm where 125 cows were milked, and I would challenge the former minister to come out to the central experimental farm with me because he cannot even milk a cow. Nor would he know how deep to put in a drill to sow an acre of wheat. Nor would he be able to plow a straight furrow.

Hamilton had been "right across Canada talking, yelling and hollering [statistics] about the condition of agriculture," but, said Hays with contempt, "statistics is for losers!" (For the official Commons record the next day, Hansard editors cleaned up Hays's grammar to read "statistics are for losers.")

"It was the first time I'd ever heard the phrase," said Keith Davey, who had been watching from the visitors' gallery. "Isn't that a great phrase? I remember when he first came down to Ottawa, and I didn't know him very well. His whole play was, look, boys, I really don't know much about this; I don't understand this stuff very well. But of course he understood it all, and that was just his way of playing it."

One press gallery reporter, Tim Creery, lent an amusing interpretation to some of what Hays said in his Commons attack. He reported that "a parliamentary milking, seeding and ploughing contest . . . may be in prospect." Hays, "butt of many an Opposition jape," had started it. Hamilton told Creery outside the Commons that he had spent ten years on western farms as a hired man; "I'd like to know of any hired man who could get away without milking a cow." But he stopped short of taking up any challenge. Creery solicited from New Democrat Arnold Peters from Temiskaming, in northern Ontario, the comment that he would be "happy to accommodate the minister." However, nothing more came of it.

Hays also used the occasion to blast one of Hamilton's most publicized farm policies, acreage payments, which Newman, too, in his book, recognized as "a straight handout." "I know there were three acreage payments made," Hays said, "and they were $200 a farm. A fat lot of good that is to a farmer in western Canada who has a $50,000 investment."

There were in Hays's remarks the beginnings of his own comprehensive agriculture program, one he had been putting quickly together from a variety of sources: his departmental advisers, his talks with provincial agriculture ministers, his visits to Europe and Russia that summer, his chats with farmers at auctions and elsewhere, his own long experience in farming. It was a program he intended should apply effectively and equitably right across the country. It was nothing daringly radical; just a little common sense at work in the head of a former barefoot boy from an Alberta barnyard. He had identified three main areas where the family farm needed help:

The cost of machinery is what is killing the family farm. You only have to go to Russia and see their system and the terrific problems they are having with production, and you will realize that the family farm is number one in importance.

The second most important thing that the farmers need is to be able to finance their farms to convert them into proper economic units. The Farm Credit Corporation [established by the Conservatives] is very good, but it does not go far enough and the lid should be taken right off [its loan limits].

Our third problem is crop disasters and taking care of the farmers when they are hailed out, dried out, blown out or frozen out.

In concluding these remarks, Hays could not refrain from revealing his deep frustration with the partisan ways of the Commons and its tedious procedures. He said dairy farmers needed more government help. "The sooner we do it the better, but how can we do it when we waste so much time in this House? The first thing we should do is take a long look at . . . the way we operate in this House. I have never seen such a waste of time. It is just fantastic."

Eight days later Hays decided, with Prime Minister Pearson's private approval, to stand and face down his tormentors in the Opposition benches over another auction he had performed. He had been particularly criticized for his absence during the Commons debate on his department's spending estimates. Pearson defended this absence by saying that Hays was out getting "in touch with the grassroots."

Provoking one of those uproars of cheering by government members on one side and jeering by Opposition members on the other for which the Commons is infamous, Hays defiantly refused to give up auctioneering for politics. He informed his detractors that he would continue auctioning cattle in the interests of promoting artificial insemination, Canadian livestock sales abroad and other worthy agricultural causes.

"Last Tuesday I left Ottawa at 11 o'clock and flew down to Kingston in a plane which I paid for," Hays said in a speech frequently interrupted by laughter, jeers from Opposition members (though not many from members representing rural Ontario ridings) and supportive cheers from government members.

I sold fifty head of cattle for fifty beef producers in Ontario who contribute to a sale each year advertising their artificial insemination units. This is a field of science which some of the honourable members here do not seem to know about. I might say that there were about seven hundred or eight hundred farmers present at this sale, and they represent the best breeders we have in Ontario.

I promised them over a year ago that I would conduct this sale for them. I have always lived up to my commitments and will continue to do so. I might say, too, that it was an excellent sale and was productive of the highest returns of any sale that has been held in eastern Ontario. The breeders were very pleased.

He defended himself further by pointing out that he had returned from the Kingston sale the same afternoon, in time to spend most of it in the Commons. In a final display of defiance to his critics, he informed them that the day before, he had conducted the all-Canadian sale, in which Conservative Senator Harry Willis had an outstanding animal, as did Dr. P. B. Rynard, a Conservative M.P. from Ontario. People had come from all over the world to buy the cattle he auctioned there, Hays pointed out. "I should like honourable members to know that we have the finest Holstein cattle in the world. I had the opportunity of selling these cattle before I became a member [of Parliament], and I am not going to stop now."

Later that day Diefenbaker found an opportunity to remark that Hays had "made a statement full of insemination and various types of personal propaganda." But by then observers of Canada's political scene from as far away as Diefenbaker's own territory of Saskatoon were becoming unimpressed with the Opposition's jokes at Hays's expense.

A few days later Hays offered a brief public glimpse of the toll his new job was taking on him. Speaking at the Carstairs Chamber of Commerce dinner held in his honour, he referred to the various challenges he had faced during his career, from learning the livestock export business to auctioneering, being mayor and now federal minister of agriculture. He admitted that the higher he rose in his work, the lonelier the life he led. "That's the price you pay for being a politician," he said. "You sit in your office in Ottawa, and your old friends aren't around. Everybody is after you for something. You sit alone and wrestle with the problems that confront you."

He had not, at least, lost his sense of humour. He recalled how he had always regretted not having more formal education. Years before, when he and his young bride had been driving past the Lethbridge federal experimental farm, he had told her: "I would have liked to have had more education, and then maybe I could have gotten a job running one of those experimental farms." Muriel had been sympathetic but encouraged him to get on as best he could where he was. Then, after he had been sworn in as minister of agriculture, she had telephoned him in Ottawa from Calgary and had asked him: "How do you expect to run those thirty-eight experimental farms now, with no education?"

A few weeks later, at a news conference in Red Deer before addressing the Alberta Liberal convention of some three hundred delegates, Hays said: "I think if I do my job, politics will take care of themselves." In a homespun speech that had delegates laughing all the way through it, he turned on his critics. "Maybe I haven't been in the House as much as I should, but I sure as hell have been in my office."

However, Hays's critics in the Commons Opposition now seemed to think they had him on the ropes. Maybe they could deliver some knockout blows when his spending estimates again came up for debate in mid-December. This Opposition attitude had been reflected in a prediction by Diefenbaker that the auctioneer-minister would soon be "going, going, gone." If Hays was worried, he showed no signs of it. He told reporters in Calgary on 5 December that he was not concerned about Diefenbaker's prediction. He then deflected it back against the Opposition leader, whose own hold on his party had slipped so badly. "Mr. Diefenbaker's position is much more precarious than mine." For good measure, he poked a little fun at his critics. "The Opposition is beginning to like me. They miss me when I'm not in the House."

The day after Hays's estimates session in the Commons, 13 December 1963, the Calgary *Herald* reported: "Agriculture Minister Harry Hays sat, mostly in silence, Thursday through one of the heaviest personal attacks ever made on a minister in the House of Commons." Ontario New Democrat Arnold Peters said: "I suggest he resign. Agriculture deserves a better deal than it is getting." Alberta Tory Jack Horner said: "Unless he spends some time in the House of Commons and in his department, becomes aware of the feeling of the average Canadian farmer, then he should spend all of his time at auctions."

Clearly, western M.P.s' concerted attacks on Hays were more political than economic. The western block of Tory M.P.s was, perhaps, disturbed that Hays was proving so beneficial to western agriculture that the record of former agriculture minister Hamilton was being blurred. Attacking the present minister was the simplest way to keep alive the image of the former one. The attacks on Hays do not appear to have represented the views of the prairie farming community, nor even the views of eastern farmers, who must have been amused by Hamilton's efforts to blame Hays for the neglect of eastern farming interests, even though Hays had been the minister for scarcely eight months.

The only moment of comfort for Hays came from fellow Albertan H. A. ("Bud") Olson. Then the Social Credit M.P. for Medicine Hat riding and later a Liberal minister of agriculture himself, he attacked Alvin Hamilton over the phony Hong Kong wheat trip, publicly revealed in Newman's just-released book. "For taking credit to himself for whatever was done, [Hamilton] is unexcelled," Olson accused. "Never before in our history has any member spent so much out of public funds in order to advertise a political party." But Hays's ordeal in the Commons that day was far from over.

Nearly two weeks earlier, he had made one of his uniquely informal speeches to the Chicago Farmers Club, a luncheon gathering of about 250 business executives who also operated farms. The meeting was in conjunction with an International Livestock Exposition, and Hays's speech included the serious message that the Canadian government was concerned over bills then before the U.S. Congress to restrict meat imports. These, Hays argued, would adversely affect Canadian farmers if enacted into law, and would also be unfair because American farm products sold in Canada amounted, proportionately, to a larger share of the total market than Canadian farm products sold in the United States.

In the course of his speech, Hays, as was his habit, had told a few rollicking tales. One of those in the audience was Frank Ryan, who farmed cattle near Canada's capital, and also owned Ottawa radio station CFRA. He had tape-recorded the speech. And somehow, back in Ottawa, the transcript had fallen into the hands of Bert Herridge, a courtly but mischievous New Democrat M.P. He chose that evening to read the speech into the Commons record. His reading was punctuated by laughter and jeering from other M.P.s. Hays, undaunted, shared in the fun. As Hays was going into his first cabinet meeting after the April election, he had been asked whether he was worried about all the high-powered farm critics he would soon be facing in the Commons Opposition ranks. Now, as this December night wore on, Hays showed what he had meant when he had replied: "I am not afraid of the dark."

Herridge opened his recital (he suggested the Farmers Club were like members of Ottawa's staid Rideau Club "in Stetson hats") with Hays's story about one of his uncles, Dan, in his home town of Carstairs.

To be the minister of agriculture, to be the mayor of a city, to be an auctioneer of a good sale or of a poor sale, you have to be a bit of an optimist, and to show you how optimistic I am about the problems of the farmers and that sort of thing, I'd like to tell you a story about an uncle of mine . . . who had guaranteed [the interest] on a couple of million dollars' worth of loans. . . . During the depression, the interest he had to pay dissipated his complete fortune.

We had a little hotel about a half-mile from the cemetery. . . . And he decided when this took place that he would go down to the hotel every morning and try to drink the beer faster than they could make it. He did this for twenty years. Every morning he was the first fellow there, and every night he was the last guy to go home . . . and he was the town gossip. Not only did everybody talk about him, but during the day he talked about everybody else. . . .

We had an old postmaster who used to go over and pick up the mail every day when the train came in at one o'clock. . . . You could set your clock by him. . . . One day he died. And they came down to the beer parlour, and someone said to this group where my uncle was partaking that day: "Say, you know Joe King died?" My uncle said, "Well, isn't that something?"

He left a will and . . . he said in his will he wanted to be buried eight feet deep. My uncle looked at it for a minute, and he finally said, "Well, I'll tell you what you do. You let them bury old Joe King eight feet down, and when I die, you just bury me two feet deep. And on resurrection day I'll be down to the beer parlour before old Joe King is at the cemetery gate."

That's the kind of an optimistic family we had.

The Chicago Farmers Club was also treated to Hays's stories about how wife Muriel's alleged lack of confidence that he could do the job had spurred him to run for mayor. Hays had said that during his first term as mayor, "I was having such a hard time they put me in easy the second time." He had gone on to explain his entry into federal politics: "Then Mr. Pearson came along and suggested maybe I should run for Parliament. If I had known what I do now— talk about the job at city hall being a tough one, this one is a lot worse. There are only about four agriculturalists in the whole Liberal party, but they are all agriculturalists on the Opposition side. So I get a good overhaul every day—every day."

Talking about the perils of grain growing in western Canada, Hays told how a farmer had a great crop one year, was hailed out the next, and "the third year he got dried out, and about that time the old lady ran away with the hired man, and he's in a real good mess, this fellow."

The swashbuckling Hays style comes through in the transcript, but not the appreciative laughter of the audience, which is audible on the tape. What his political opponents still had to learn was that, at a speaker's podium, Hays gave off an infectious energy that suffused his spoken words with more humour than they retained when written down. He spoke with a twinkle in his voice as well as in his eyes. The Chicago audience obviously appreciated Hays's bucolic charm more than Herridge realized. Canadian audiences would soon show a similar appreciation for the platform talent of the cabinet bumpkin, just as was beginning to happen to some in his audience that night in the Commons and in the press gallery above.

Reporter Tim Creery, for instance, had taken to calling Hays "Head-on Harry" as a reflection of what he saw as Hays's awkwardness in the Commons. The morning after Herridge's performance, Creery wrote in the Calgary *Herald:*

> For the first time since the former Mayor of Calgary became an M.P., the House heard the authentic Hays. In the Commons he has been awkward, stilted and obviously uncomfortable. But among his fellow big-time agricultural entrepreneurs of the Chicago Farmers Club on Dec. 2, he was himself—down-to-earth, ribald, ungrammatical, ebullient, optimistic and enjoying himself.

Creery's report ended: "Hays had one consolation. At the conclusion of Herridge's reading, his Chicago speech got prolonged desk-thumping applause and cheering from the Liberal benches."

When he at last got the floor, Hays did not refer directly to Herridge's prolonged fun-poking, but rather dealt with it obliquely:

I hope everybody had a great deal of fun here this evening. Certainly, I have provided some of it. I am thankful of that. All through my life, I have had a great admiration for people who do things, and I would like honourable members to know that it is a great challenge to me to be minister of agriculture. I do not have as much book learning as a lot of people have, but I have a sense of responsibility, and I can contribute to agriculture.

First thing the next morning, Hays flew home to Calgary to speak to some six hundred delegates at a Farmers' Union of Alberta convention. Before he spoke, he was interviewed by the Calgary *Herald.* "Quit?" Hays responded to the reporter's question. "Hell! I'm just getting to like this job."

He did not consider that he had been given a rough time in the Commons the previous day. He told the *Herald:*

In the five and a half hours they talked about my department, nobody attacked the department. They just made a lot of personal attacks on me. They tell you you have to be thick-skinned in this business. I just consider where these attacks are coming from. I suppose there are a lot of people who would like me to quit, but not in my party and, I hope, not in my department.

The audience awaiting him was a critical and skeptical one, as Hays knew. This was his first appearance, since becoming agriculture minister, before any western farmers' union convention. He had missed their conventions in Saskatchewan and Manitoba, and their farmer members considered this a snub, even though Hays had said official business kept him from attending both. The mood he could expect had been reflected in a comment by Alberta Farmers' Union President Ed Nelson: "If Hays had not shown up, his whole political future would have been wiped out."

Hays spent a good part of his speech describing the ideas for new and revised farm policies that he had begun to develop in his first Commons speech. But it was the way he dealt with the widely publicized attacks on him in the Commons the day before that most impressed his farm audience in the end. As he had told the *Herald,* he said he was "elated" because none of the Opposition criticism had been directed at his department, only at him.

During a wide-ranging question period after his speech, Hays was asked how he felt about Prime Minister Pearson "taking the Wheat Board away from you." Hays replied: "I don't care what they do as long as it works good, and it is working good." He was applauded.

The following day, 14 December 1963, the Edmonton *Journal* reported that Hays "drew a generally favourable reaction" from the farmers' union delegates. The new union president, Paul Babey, said Hays seemed straightforward in his answers and appeared to by trying awfully hard to do well in his position. Several delegates referred to Hays's previous occupation as an auctioneer. "Only an auctioneer," said one, "could have gotten through so much information so quickly." Another delegate said: "He's a flamboyant westerner who is apt to flounder his way into some pretty good legislation before he is through."

About a week later, in Diefenbaker's old stamping ground, a Saskatoon *Star-Phoenix* editorial declared that it was time to give Hays "a big, hearty western pat on the back" for his role as federal minister of agriculture. It believed the retransfer of the Canadian Wheat Board to trade minister Mitchell Sharp, and the apparent cooperation between him and Hays, was a welcome feature of cabinet solidarity. The editorial concluded with laudatory prose that made sweet reading for Hays.

> Canadian farmers are lucky that Mr. Hays is the Minister of Agriculture, that his strength is in his economic success rather than meaningless political prowess on the floor of the Commons. On purely political grounds those who criticize Mr. Hays show little wisdom. Those highly paid M.P.s might profit by Mr. Hays' example, and get along with the nation's business. He's earning his pay. It's doubtful if as much can be said for all those M.P.s who think they could do a better job than Mr. Hays.

It was as good a note as any on which Hays could close out that year.

CHAPTER TEN

THE
POWER OF
SPEECHES

Harry Hays had always found it troublesome to read speeches prepared by hired speech writers; he was more accustomed to using sketchy notes, as often as not put down by his own hand.

The first time Keith Davey heard Hays speak in public, they were on a platform at the Red Deer annual meeting of Alberta Liberals in the fall of 1963, a few months after Hays had become the most powerful Liberal in the province. Hays kept glancing down at a file folder on the podium in front of him. "He had his notes written in a circle and he kept turning the folder as he spoke," Davey recalled. "It was like a record playing from the inside out—the circle kept getting larger." When Hays had slowly turned the folder in a complete circle, his speech was finished, and he sat down.

In February of 1964 Jim Coutts, appointments secretary for Prime Minister Pearson, telephoned me in the Parliamentary Press Gallery, where I was then the Ottawa correspondent of Toronto radio station CHUM, and invited me to lunch with him at the National Press Club. Over our meal he asked me if I would be interested in becoming Hays's special assistant, responsible for handling his relations with the news media and writing material for his statements and speeches.

Coutts extended his offer at the right time. I had come to feel that I had been sitting in smug, unresponsible judgement of the politicians in the Commons arena below my press gallery desk for too long, and perhaps it was time to put my money where my mouth was.

I had never met Harry Hays, even though we were natives of the same province, so Coutts introduced us a few days later. Hays seemed as wary of me as I was of relinquishing the position of influence I imagined my press gallery job afforded me. But I could detect no bad vibrations, and as we talked, I sensed a certain warmth and energy about Hays that I thought would probably make working with him tolerable. My references apparently satisfied him, and we agreed that I would come to work for him in April 1964, about a year after his election.

I was not altogether ignorant of agriculture. During my youth in Alberta I had milked my family's few cows and had helped in the grain harvest for a few farmers, including Harry Strom, later premier of Alberta. From the press gallery I had written about agriculture for the Canadian Press and the *Financial Post* before joining the urban-focussed CHUM. On my first trip with Hays, a weekend foray to Calgary, he completely swamped me with an unbroken stream of new information about every aspect of agriculture. Agriculture began to take on a whole new meaning for me, as did the political process that made possible the opportunity to improve the lot of Canada's farmers.

Our early experiences with my formally written speeches were more painful than either of us had anticipated. But we got better as we went along, until we both found ourselves enjoying, more than either of us had expected to, the impact that speeches could have on the power game of politics. Words, Hays discovered, contained the power to change not only his public image but also, given a little time, the public's thoughts on policies.

Our first joint speech effort was for use at a farm forum in Strathmore, Alberta, in May 1963. It comprised about a dozen pages of notes summarizing what had been happening in agriculture since Hays became minister, and a few sentences about national unity, then, Hays recognized, a hot political issue, especially in Quebec. "I think," it had him saying, "farmers in all parts of this country understand as well as any other section of the population how important it is that Canada remains one country." Once on the platform, however, Hays decided to wing it, as he was accustomed to doing, and he never used his notes.

We faced a challenge of a different sort with our next speech effort. This was to be a full-length oration for a much larger and more crucial occasion—a meeting in Saskatoon in support of the Liberal candidate in a by-election there, Sid Buckwold, who was fresh from a successful stint as Saskatoon's mayor.

Hays's aversion to reading his speech texts was due largely to his poor eyesight; he had difficulty following a typed manuscript. So for this next speech text, some tricks of the broadcasting trade were employed. The lines were kept short, which made the text easier to follow. Each sentence was a separate paragraph, and several dots, instead of commas, separated the phrases. Each page ended with a complete sentence, to prevent Hays stumbling if he had any trouble turning the page. Lastly, the text was printed in larger than usual type.

There was only one problem with this approach. So few lines could be put on a page that a lot of pages were needed, even for a short speech—in this case, a stack of thirty-four sheets for a twenty-minute speech. And when we arrived in Saskatoon, we discovered this was going to be more of a problem than anticipated. We had expected the meeting to be held in the Bessborough Hotel. Instead, it was to be held in a park beside the South Saskatchewan River. Hays would have to deliver his speech from the raised bandstand in the middle of the park, without even the use of a podium.

He stood behind a stand-up microphone and clutched his fistful of pages in both hands. By the time he started to speak, a light wind had come up. I sat nearby, worrying about which the wind would carry off first—Hays's text or his brown fedora. But he soldiered on through page after page, stumbling now and then over phrasing or pronunciation, but forging ahead as though nothing had happened, until he had delivered the whole bundle, pages and hat intact.

All that effort failed to help poor Buckwold, however; he lost the by-election.

In late August 1964 Hays hosted a Canadian visit by his Soviet Union counterpart, Ivan P. Volovchenko. The Soviet agriculture minister had accepted Hays's invitation, made during his Russian visit the previous year, to tour across Canada to study Canadian farming methods. Volovchenko and his party spent some time in Ottawa before visiting other parts of Ontario, Quebec and then the prairies. Merely a courtesy visit, it had no immediate concrete or policy results.

Volovchenko was heavy-set and slightly taller than average with a plain but friendly poker face. Four shining gold upper incisors flashed when he smiled. He seldom removed his dark fedora. He and his Moscow companions—including a bull-chested fellow who we Canadians suspected was the KGB watchdog—gave few indications that they were impressed by the productivity of the Canadian farms they visited. However, one of our party understood their language quite well, and he soon had no doubt that they were impressed. He would often overhear them marvelling among themselves: how surprising they found it, for instance, that such a large wheat farm as the one we visited in the Regina area, some two thousand acres, could be operated by only the farmer and his wife.

We travelled in a cavalcade of four cars. A part of our nightly accommodation arrangements, personally approved by Hays, provided for a hospitality room, where everyone could gather for a drink at the end of a long day. Initially, we arranged to have plenty of vodka available. But we quickly realized that the Soviets preferred beer or rye and ginger ale. So we changed the fluids balance, and our Soviet guests enjoyed the nightly gatherings as much as their Canadian hosts did.

Among the Soviet party was Victoria Khoroshilov, the daughter of the Russian agriculture attaché to Canada and the interpreter for Volovchenko. She was full of youthful curiosity wherever we went. The night we spent in Swift Current, Saskatchewan, a few of us strolled along its main street. At one point she fell into pace alongside me and remarked, in a rare moment of Soviet candour, how different it was taking a walk at night in a Canadian city than in a Russian city. Here everyone left all the lights on; it was bright and cheerful. At home only a few lights were left on; it was dark and gloomy.

At Calgary, Hays assumed leadership of the tour. In a rented car, he drove Volovchenko around his ranch and that of his neighbour, James Allen Baker. He took gleeful pleasure in leading the accompanying journalists a merry chase through fields of fender-high grass usually travelled only on foot or by horseback. Once, they stopped to examine a field of wheat lying in swath. The Russian minister marvelled at its obvious heavy yield. It was the best he had ever seen. Hays grinned and explained that it was Yugo winter wheat, a Russian variety he had obtained as seed from a nearby Hutterite colony.

When the party paused another time during the ranch visit, a band of curious quarter horses trotted over to investigate. As Hays described their virtues to Volovchenko, Khoroshilov interpreted. She suddenly burst into laughter. "They're sensible and strong," Hays had said. "They can carry a fat man like me without tiring."

□   □   □

By the autumn of 1964 reporters and columnists in the Parliamentary Press Gallery were having serious second thoughts about Hays—and, more importantly for him, were publishing them.

Hays then had a two-pronged bill before the Commons, to expand the size of loans available to farmers from the government's Farm Credit Corporation, and to provide for three or more farmers together to form syndicates and borrow as a group to buy machinery for shared use. He was fighting the bill's Opposition critics with an effectiveness that caught the attention of his home-town morning newspaper. For Hays, the *Albertan*'s editorial was deeply satisfying, coming after all the censure he had been taking from the likes of Alvin Hamilton, Peter Newman and others.

> Hays needs no help from us in his fight against Progressive Conservative forces who would, if they could, sidetrack his farm loan bill

. . . In fact it would seem safe to suggest that Mr. Hays is in need of help from no one. As the Tories are discovering to their cost, Mr. Hays is no longer, as some implied in the beginning, the overalls-clad hick from the political sticks, the unsure groping parliamentary neophyte. Instead, he is a progressively maturing sophisticate who has confidence in his grasp of the problems confronting the Canadian agricultural scene and his ability to cope with them.

Edmonton Tory Terry Nugent had attempted to kill the bill; Hays blasted him in the Commons, calling his move "the cheapest kind of two-bit partisan politics" aimed at defeating the government and forcing another election on Canadians, and asked rhetorically: "Is this what the leader of the Opposition means when he says he wants action?"

Before the parliamentary day was out, several more Tories had felt the sting of what the *Albertan* called the "minister's shining new verbal quiver." "Mr. Hays has come of age both as a member of Parliament and minister of the crown, passing from the role of an able defence to one of courageous and devastating offence."

Canadian Press correspondent Arch MacKenzie reported that since entering the Commons as "a political tenderfoot," Hays had "faced one of the most ornery bands of hombres ever to draw on a greenhorn minister. . . . There were times when Mr. Hays appeared to have his trigger finger jammed in his six-shooter. However, he is steadily gaining a surer touch and the capacity to give as good as he gets on any day in Parliament."

His bill was unanimously approved in principle. A lengthy profile of Hays in the Toronto *Star* in October 1964 commented:

> As fresh as the rain falling on prairie wheat fields, the minister is an exhilarating addition to the drought-stricken political landscape. Whether he is trying to weed out of his department two gardeners assigned to potted plants in cabinet ministers' offices or supervising his ministry's million dollar a day budget, Harry Hays has a bullheaded charm.

About questions from the Opposition, Hays was quoted using his characteristic bluntness: "The questions I get are generally stupid, and stupid questions sometimes have to have stupid answers. Thus both the questioner and the answerer look stupid."

The *Star* article went on to say that there were occasions when Hays's directness was certainly no hindrance to the subtlety of his intellect. Hays's perceptiveness was apparent during an Ottawa meeting of a consultative committee formed by Canadian and U.S. cabinet ministers. Hays sat through Finance Minister Walter Gordon's speech without appearing to be especially attentive. But at the end of the meeting he gave Gordon a detailed analysis of what he had said and of the American reaction. He had been watching carefully to see which points had impressed them and which had not. On the basis of Hays's observations, Gordon was able to re-cast the Canadian presentation and at the following meeting stress those aspects that had not caught the Americans' attention.

The agriculture minister's time was not wholly occupied with his political career. He still found the opportunity to slip away to his ranch for an occasional weekend, saddle a couple of horses and go riding for hours on end with Muriel; it was one of his favourite relaxations. He also bought some driving ponies and a minibuggy and would sometimes take Muriel out in that rig for a ride across the ranch lands. Every summer, too, there was some auctioneering to do at the Calgary Exhibition and Stampede. And of course there was the annual Hays Stampede breakfast, every year more and more of a Calgary tradition.

Prime Minister Pearson and his wife, Maryon, joined the break-fast celebrants in the summer of 1964. By then it attracted some 3500 guests. In part because of Hays's growing national fame, but more so because of the prime minister's presence, the breakfast goings-on that July also attracted substantial national publicity. A National Film Board crew filmed the tumultuous scene from a heli-copter. A front-page headline in the next morning's Toronto *Globe and Mail* read: "Pre-Stampede Breakfast Bash Held at Harry's Home on the Range: Out West Where the Stetsons Swirl . . . and Eggs Are Scrambled in 10-Gallon Cans."

A team of about 250 volunteers, many of them Hays's fellow Rotarians and not a few of them top Calgary businessmen, had been busily preparing the breakfast food since 3 A.M. Forty cooks scrambled 450 dozen eggs in ten-gallon cans and used shovels to scoop them off the cooking griddles. Served up with the eggs were 480 pounds of sausages, 1500 pounds of fried potatoes, 250 dozen rolls and dozens of gallons of coffee. By then, too, fifteen cases each of forty-eight-ounce tins of orange and grapefruit juice, fortified with unstated amounts of gin, had been offered to the guests. "Get it now while the bugs are still on top," the juice dispensers liked to shout.

By the time the Pearsons arrived about eight in the morning, he wearing the required Stetson, and she a wide country-style skirt with running shoes, the Klondike Six band had been belting out "When the Saints Go Marching In" for an hour. Soon half a dozen bands, preparing for the parade next morning, were struggling to be heard over the skirl of bagpipes, the rattle of a honky-tonk piano, the strain of an ancient calliope and the sounds of a dozen other instruments. Another world heavyweight boxing champion, Rocky Marciano, was present, along with John Russell, star of the television series *The Lawman.*

Prime Minister Pearson grinned down from the back of a truck, where he and Maryon had been directed, the better to see and to be seen. "I don't normally have this kind of experience on Sunday. I am usually getting ready to go to church about this time." Instead of church, he witnessed the traditional climax of the breakfast party—Hays mixing his batch of sillabub.

Wearing his familiar fringed buckskin jacket and the pink cowboy hat that had grey pigtails stuffed with dollar bills dangling from it, Hays proceeded to pour a concoction of mostly alcoholic liquids from a collection of old shoe polish, hand lotion and patent medicine bottles and tins into a large hollow carved in a huge block of ice.

Hays's Stampede breakfast patter as he mixed the sillabub followed a similar pattern year after year, but it still drew laughs from the crowd. As he poured in the ingredients, he would make familiar claims for the potion's rare qualities of rejuvenation. "Many women eighty years old who drank this were confined before Christmas. A lot of these young girls don't know what I'm talking about. This is the age of the Pill." He would nod at various friends standing close by, signalling them to help. "Now, we'll put in the base here." And they would pour in several bottles of gin. "Now a little laxative and a little iodine. And a dash of Windex. We gotta keep things clean. Oh, and Muriel is going to toss in a little stuff we couldn't get rid of last year."

A young jersey cow was then led up between two pipers. "This morning we have a bilingual cow. She was born on the forty-ninth parallel between Ontario and Quebec. She has four faucets and they all work. She gives skim milk, cream, cottage cheese and bleu cheese." Hays milked fresh milk from her into a bowl and handed it to Pearson to pour in with the other ingredients.

"Dangedest thing I've ever seen," Hays said as the Pearsons bent over the ice bowl with him. "It's boiling. Wonderful. I can tell by the smiles of the grandmothers here that it worked last year." Maryon Pearson's only comment on Hays's sillabub when she sipped it was a grimace that evoked from him a wide grin. Then he looked out at the crowd and invited: "All right, all you old girls who haven't had any fun for a long time, come and get some. All you people who want to be saved, step right up."

□   □   □

At the beginning of his federal political career, Hays had taken great pains never to be associated with public criticism of John Diefenbaker, because of his popularity on Hays's home turf in Calgary. He gradually became so disgusted with the former prime minister's tactics, though, that in November 1964 he tackled Diefenbaker head-on. He chose as his vehicle a speech to the annual meeting of the Toronto and District Liberal Association. The speech summed up the tragedy of Diefenbaker's political career— for Canadians who had invested so much hope and belief in him as well as for himself—with accuracy, perception and now and then a touch of humour. It proved to be one of Hays's most widely quoted speeches: the Quebec City *Chronical-Telegraph,* for instance, ran the whole text as a three-part series, and several other newspapers ran excerpts.

The speech started with a not-so-subtle dig at the straw-in-the-teeth image Alvin Hamilton had cultivated while serving as Diefenbaker's agriculture minister. "In my days as a cattle showman and auctioneer," Hays began,

> I have slept in the best barns the Royal has to offer. I mean the Royal Winter Fair, of course—not the Royal York Hotel. But I don't want to present myself as a country bumpkin or a hayseed, whatever political advantages that folksy image may have seemed to have for one of my recent predecessors. . . . I don't believe you have to pose

as a country cousin with barnyard on your overalls or even as a farm hand . . . to do a decent job as minister of agriculture.

Hays then took up a line of that political faint praise that damns, a tack he had first tried in a speech a couple of weeks earlier which tried to overcome anti-Liberal sentiment among western farmers with a dose of unusually nonpartisan self-critical political candour.

I think the last Liberal government had forgotten the farmers during its declining years. I'll even go further—I think that on the basis of its record with the farmers, the last Liberal government deserved to be kicked out when it was. I am what I am in federal politics today only because I was convinced that this is a Liberal government that is not like the last Liberal government. We have tried to show the same kind of concern for our farmers under the present government as was shown by the previous government. I won't take anything away from them on that score. They did things for our farmers that should have been done long before. My only objection is that they only went half as far as they should have.

Now, to his large audience of Toronto Liberals, Hays took up this theme again as he proceeded to attack Hamilton, without mentioning him by name.

One of my most interesting discoveries since becoming minister of agriculture—and believe me, I've made quite a few since April of 1963—has been just who was responsible for all the major farm programs of the previous administration. It was not the man whose brilliant and imaginative image-maker so successfully inflated his reputation to the dimensions of a latter-day saint of the back forty.

Hays's friend and fellow Calgarian Doug Harkness had been minister of agriculture under Diefenbaker before Hamilton. It was during this time that the Agricultural Prices Stabilization Board was established, the Crop Insurance Administration was introduced, the Farm Credit Corporation was established and work was begun on legislation to establish the ARDA (Agricultural Rehabilitation and Development Act) program. Hays believed the Tory farm program to be a good one, but, he said again, it had not gone far enough.

Hays could have pointed to his own legislation for farm improvements, but instead he widened his attack to include Diefenbaker, whom he described as "a kind of super medicine man, with a wagonload of miracle potions and a pitchman's empty spiel."

There are many sad, even tragic, chapters in the story of Canada's Diefenbaker years. There is a large element of tragedy in the story of Mr. Diefenbaker himself, a tragedy that involves him personally, a tragedy that involves the Conservative party and a tragedy that involves the Canadian people.

His personal tragedy lies in the fact that he won a greater measure of confidence from the Canadian people than any prime minister in our history, then dropped the reins and finally fell right out of the saddle before his horse ever got away from the corral.

The tragedy for the Conservative party was that the Diefenbaker government, with the biggest majority in history, could have accomplished anything it set out to accomplish for the people of Canada. Instead, said Hays, it either failed to see what needed to be done or, seeing the problems, could not decide how to solve them.

I think Canada needs the Conservative party. Even if it has never done terribly well as a government since the days of Sir John A. Macdonald, it has served the country reasonably well in the role of Opposition. But I quite honestly fear that if Mr. Diefenbaker goes on the way he has lately . . . the Conservative party may even lose this role in Canadian affairs. . . . Frankly, I have given up on him completely.

For the Canadian people the tragedy was that they had trusted Diefenbaker, yet he had let them down. "Instead of a prime minister," Hays said, "they discovered they had elected a performer, and a pretty stagey and theatrical performer at that. The Diefenbaker kingdom—for a little while so vast and promising—now lies in ruins, and he brought it all about by himself."

Neither Diefenbaker nor Hamilton ever showed any sign that they unduly resented what Hays had said Criticism of opponents was part of the gamesmanship of politics—a gamesmanship the seasoned politician understands very well. Although Hays could look more benignly on his political opponents the longer he remained on Parliament Hill, he had truly come to believe what he had said about Diefenbaker. Simply from observing the former prime minister in the Commons, Hays had concluded, as his Toronto speech indicated, that Diefenbaker was nothing more than a rhetoric-ridden political opportunist with no decisive convictions about how to solve any of Canada's most pressing challenges, from language rights to farm policies. He once, in private, likened Diefenbaker to a mischievous dog always trying to dig up someone else's flower garden or tear holes in a fence—always destructive, never constructive.

From his abrasive experience as a cabinet minister, Hays gradually came to hold a view of politics and politicians similar to my own—a view we eventually concluded is in accord with the fundamental reality of democratic politics and government. It is a view perhaps best described as humanistic rather than idealistic, and it is certainly a long way from mystical. This shared political view was one of the enduring bases of our working relationship. There was nothing unique about it, and once arrived at, it seemed eminently obvious as only common sense. However, for many with political interests, this concept of politics is not always as self-evident as more idealistic—Hays would have said unrealistic—expectations.

This political view had evolved, for me, out of my gradual accumulation of experience as a parliamentary reporter. In making fair and reasonable judgements of politicians and their works, I had to equate the human factor in that judgement. As a journalist, I achieved perfection with great infrequency, given that I had to grapple with my own human factor. What right had I to write about politicians' performances, demanding higher standards for them than I expected to be demanded of me in my work? Hays had come to take a similar attitude towards the voters: if they have any sense of realism and fairness, he said, they should not expect more of their politicians than they do of themselves, especially now that he knew from personal experience what it was really like inside politics and government—how utterly ridden with human factors the inner rooms behind the closed doors really were. The best kept secret in government, Hays believed, is how little goes on there that needs to be kept secret.

A speech Hays made to the largely conservative Calgary Chamber of Commerce in March 1965 reflected this new lesson from his experience as a newcomer to Parliament and the cabinet. Hays was deeply impressed with how different government looked from the inside than it did from the outside. "When you see all these clashing interests coming at you from all directions," he said, "it's enough to turn anybody into a damn socialist." His speech candidly told what it was like to be in power, and how there were no political machines, but only ordinary individuals trying to do their best for their constituents and their country. It was another speech that attracted, for Hays, a very satisfying level of news media attention.

Whenever I come back to Calgary from Ottawa, I still feel like a traveller returning from a very strange land. . . .

Three qualities are essential to survive in federal politics—even at the backbencher level: an iron constitution; a great, big, fat ego that can live on its own self-esteem, and a hide as thick as a Brahma bull's after twenty winters. If you want to survive as a cabinet minister, you also need a powerful governor on your temper. Otherwise, you'd tell everybody what they could do with their job the second or third day in office.

You soon realize that when all the problems of government are boiled down, what you've been elected to deal with is power—the political power assigned to Parliament by the people of this country. It can be a lonely and frightening realization. It's like dreaming you were suddenly assigned to referee the Stanley Cup playoffs—and then woke up to find the dream had come true. The first time you look out over the Canadian public from the high and windy slopes of Parliament Hill, I don't think anybody could blame you for thinking it's like a vast sea of clamour.

You're hardly inside your new office before requests and demands for everything you can imagine start flying at you from all directions—followed by criticism and abuse because you didn't give everybody everything he wants the day before yesterday. Your first impulse is to duck under your desk and never come out, or sneak out the rear door and go back to Pekisko Creek. But you don't want all your friends, or your critics, to discover that underneath you're no more a hero than anybody else. So you stay there and try to deal with things as best you can, and after awhile you begin to see a little order in all the chaos. . . .

Being in government does give you a new respect for the Canadian people. . . . In spite of everything their governments, and their Oppositions, do, they still go on surviving and building a better Canada, and sometimes even prospering while they're at it.

A cabinet minister hears from the Canadian public in a variety of ways. You get letters by the bushel. If a person is sore, he might send you a telegram. And if he is really outraged, he'll call you by telephone—sometimes collect if he can get away with it, or come right down to Ottawa and bang on your office door. But that's the gentle side of a cabinet minister's life.

Where he really gets his lumps is from the Opposition in the House of Commons, and from his warm, friendly, helpful, considerate fellow government supporters at the weekly caucus. The Opposition criticize you for everything, and of course their job is to criticize. But it's a mistake to expect much from your own people, either. Most of them figure, at least privately, although sometimes publicly, too, that anything their ministers can do, they could do better, if they only had a chance.

I used to go home some nights after I first got to Ottawa with eggs sticking out all over my skull. There were so many at one point, I even thought of naming them, like a mountain range—Diefenbaker, Jack Horner, Eldon Woolliams, Lawrence Kindt, Peter Newman. But I guess the only way some people can learn is to have it beaten into them and now that some of the lessons I had to learn are beginning to trickle through the bone, I'm not a bit sorry I decided to go into politics.

My two years as a cabinet minister have been a whole new experience for me—a whole new education. . . . There are no magic machines hidden away in cabinet backrooms where you just put in your quarter, press a button and out comes a neatly packaged policy kit. The initial source of every government action is the same as it has always been—that imperfect wonder of the world, the human mind.

Hays then turned to what he had come to believe was one of the most self-deceiving political myths that Albertans, and particularly Calgarians, habitually indulged in—the myth of being Canada's, and maybe the world's, greatest private enterprisers. The Alberta private enterprise myth was founded on an unquestioning faith that

humans in private business have access to supranatural entre-
preneurial and management skills that are inaccessible to humans in
government. Implicit in this myth is the belief that everything done
by private business is automatically right and everything done by
government is automatically wrong.

Hays had learned by then that there had always been as much
assistance from the federal and provincial governments to the Alberta economy as in any other province, and more often than not in
answer to demands from the business community.

One of the considerations behind this part of Hays's speech was
his growing concern about the obsessive opposition from Alberta's
exceedingly conservative and influential Social Credit Premier
Ernest Manning to the Pearson government's medicare plan, then
being negotiated with the provincial governments. One of Manning's lines of attack was to suggest that the plan was socialistic
because the federal offer to split the cost with each provincial government was conditional on universal coverage. This made participation in medicare insurance mandatory for all citizens. Manning,
alone among the premiers, wanted coverage to be on a voluntary
means-test subsidy basis—a basis that extensive research by a
Diefenbaker-appointed royal commission had indicated was vastly
less workable than the Pearson plan.

The complex paradox that Manning could not grasp was that individual freedom of access to equal medical treatment, at minimum
cost, could only be achieved if every Canadian were required to
participate, to ensure that all qualified for this freedom when
chance ill health demanded it. This, the royal commission had concluded, was also the most financially efficient method for Canada to
provide equality of access to medical treatment.

Hays was trying, in a very indirect way, to offset some of Manning's attack on the plan—an attack which was destined to become
an increasingly large political problem for Hays in his home riding.

He began this part of his speech by saying that, despite his own
experience in governing, he no longer knew what the Opposition
meant when they used words like "socialistic" and "all the old clin-
kers about free enterprise" as diversionary tactics in their attacks
on the government's medicare legislation. He continued:

We don't have any herd books or brand registers down in Ottawa, where you can look up the political bloodlines of a policy and find out whether it's Liberal or Conservative or Socialistic or Social Credit. As far as I can tell, a government just tries to assess what the problems are and then tries to figure out how to cope with them. . . .

The other day, one of my more educated friends called me a pragmatist. I didn't know whether to be insulted or take it as a compliment. So I just nodded and kept quiet until I could get to a dictionary and look it up. I found that a pragmatist is someone who judges everything by its practical application to human interest. In other words, a practical man who just tries to get along with the facts of life as they are rather than as he might wish they were.

It seems to me this is what every government has to be when it gets right down to the country's problems. I think every government that tried to run things any other way has finally run into trouble. So I think we have to be careful when we start throwing political labels around.

Hays pointed out that, in the eyes of the rest of Canada, Alberta was considered a hotbed of political reactionaries. This surprised him, he said, because he had always found Albertans as open-minded and as ready to take a chance as people anywhere else in Canada. But he feared the problem Albertans had was that they saw themselves "as the last of a dying breed . . . the last of the red-hot free enterprisers." He argued that Canada had never been a purely free enterprise country at all.

The economic foundation of Canada from its very beginning has always been a combination of government enterprise and private enterprise and I think it's time we all stopped kidding ourselves about this. . . . Anyone who cares to look at the facts will discover, as I have discovered, that right here in Alberta, a lot of us private enterprisers owe an awful lot of our present prosperity not to free enterprise but to government enterprise—to governments that listened to the needs of the people who elected them. . . .

How much irrigated farm land and how many prosperous irrigation farmers would we have in Alberta today if it weren't for government enterprise? . . . That fortress of free enterprisers, the CPR, would never have spanned the prairies and the Rocky Mountains if government enterprise hadn't made it possible. . . .

Are old age pensions "socialistic"—or just good, civilized government policy? Is it socialism or just civilized social justice to provide family allowances, unemployment insurance, workmen's compensation, hospital insurance? What about government credit for farmers? For our export trade? Is this threatening our banks with socialism? Or is it just using our national resources to do what private resources either can't or don't want to do? . . .

My point is not that governments can solve all our problems, or should even be expected to. But some of our problems can only be tackled by the combined resources of us all, and the best way we have yet devised for that kind of co-operation—in spite of their many obvious imperfections—is through our governments. . . . I mention these things, not to advocate more government enterprise in our affairs, but because I think we need more clear thinking about the whole role of government in our nation today.

This was intended as a message of simple political realism, a friendly reminder of what Hays thought was self-evident: government must, inevitably, play a key role in any economy, including the private enterprise economy of Alberta. Only government was able to set and enforce the rules of the economic game. The real issue was not *whether* there should be government intervention in the economy; it was the purpose and quality of that intervention. Albertans, however, were far from ready in 1965 to listen seriously to such a message.

CHAPTER ELEVEN

RESPONSES AND REACTIONS

Calgary historian-journalist James H. Gray was in the audience at Harry Hays's Calgary Chamber of Commerce speech in March 1965. A few days later he marvelled in the Montreal *Star* at "the shattering metamorphosis" of the agriculture minister. "Two years ago, Mr. Hays decamped for Ottawa in the scratchiest hairshirt since Diogenes," he wrote, "the most truculently reluctant successful politician of the election. He left the impression that he had been conned into this thing, and that the Ottawa politicians and bureaucrats had better watch their steps or he would be out of politics and back in Calgary."

He came home to Calgary last week a man so changed that some of his beholders refused to believe their ears. . . . It was clear to all

that Harry Hays is now in politics to stay. . . . Standing by themselves in his prepared text, [his] words looked trite, platitudinous,
corny. But when spoken by Harry Hays, his words had never carried
more conviction. . . . They were convincing because he believed
them, and he believed them because he had obviously discovered
satisfactions in life far beyond anything to which a dollar sign could be
attached. . . .

The pragmatic Harry Hays may well be a fellow his oldline Calgary
supporters have a little trouble adjusting to. He's far from the Harry
Hays they used to know.

By this time Hays's reputation as an entertaining and provocative
platform performer had spread, as columnist Richard Jackson confirmed in the Sudbury *Star* a month later under the headline:
" 'Homespun Harry' has magic by which campaigns are won."

It's getting so that good old plain-talkin' Harry Hays, our folksy,
new-type, down-to-earth Agriculture Minister, has hardly a minute
to himself these days. He's just the hottest political platform
performer on Parliament Hill, dispensing a special personal kind of
homespun, down-on-the-farm politics that can't be matched this side
of the Beverly Hillbillies. He's in wild demand by every Liberal M.P.
who wants to make his annual constituency meeting or pre-election
rally something the voters will write into their memory books.

There was the time that Ol' Alvin Hamilton . . . used to be the
parliamentary pin-up boy. And for a time Trade Minister Mitchell
Sharp—Sharp Mitchell, his fans call him—was shaping up as the
Crown Prince of the Commons. . . . Harry Hays is selling something
far more basic, and maybe that's why he's every M.P.'s nomination
for Best Guest Speaker back in the riding.

In February, Hays had given a speech to the annual meeting in
Toronto of the Holstein-Friesian Association of Canada, in which he
expounded on his extensive revisions to federal financial support
for farm exhibitions and to their competition classifications. What
caught everyone's attention was his reference to a new interbreed
category of best udder for dairy cows.

Hays knew that the cost of competing in the farm sections of
shows such as the Pacific National Exhibition in Vancouver, the

Exhibition and Stampede in Calgary and the Canadian National Exhibition in Toronto had risen sharply, and that consequently many farmers were finding participation increasingly difficult. He had also decided that another major reason for declining spectator interest was the profusion of categories; one had to sit too long in the stands waiting for the classes one was particularly interested in seeing.

Hays was most concerned, though, about the declining emphasis on utility in the exhibition classifications. Part of this concern stemmed from his observations as an auctioneer that fat beef animals were still being marketed when the consumer trend was towards lean diets. Since long before Hays became minister of agriculture, he had made it his habit to buy prime rib roast out of the championship beef steer at the annual Royal Winter Fair in Toronto. More often than not, he had found this prize-winning meat disappointingly over-fat. So along with reducing the number of prize classifications and increasing the prize money for those that survived, Hays introduced to the new beef steer championship category the factor of carcass leanness after slaughter.

In Hays's view, an agricultural exhibition was never intended to be a "fashion show for shapely young heifers or beautiful cows or pretty pigs." Agriculture, he held, was concerned with the business of producing food, and to Hays the loveliest sight in agriculture was an animal that produced the most food in the shortest time and with the lowest feed intake.

As an example of the inutility of farm fair measurements, Hays often raised the case of Shropshire sheep. They were great to look at, he said, with their darling, wool-covered faces. The trouble was that in a Canadian winter, the wool froze over their eyes so they could neither see grass to eat nor find their way home from the pasture. Sometimes they would wander blindly until they froze to death, to their owner's loss. Hays wanted to put production performance ahead of such useless prettiness in the exhibition competitions.

In his speech to the Holstein-Friesian dairy breeders, Hays acknowledged that the interbreed best udder category he was proposing in his farm fairs package was creating the most controversy. He had learned this during many meetings with the various breed associations to hammer out the new package. Guernsey dairy farmers did not object to contesting the udders of other Guernseys, or Jerseys other Jerseys, or Ayrshires other Ayrshires, but not Guernsey against Jersey, Ayrshire and Holstein.

With what he next said, Hays was lucky that the women's rights movement was still some years away from its zenith.

Concern has been expressed that this new interbreed class might cause disharmony among our dairy breeds. I've been told it's an over-simplification of a very complicated situation to say "An udder is an udder, and it doesn't matter to what kind of cow it is attached." With all due respect to women and dairy cows, I think the same argument applies with about as much validity to some of our beauty contests. I realize that a lot more could be said on the subject, but isn't an ankle an ankle, a bosom a bosom, whether the girl is Canadian or Swedish or from Australia? After all, a cow's equipment, just like a woman's, is intended to do a certain job, and the most important part of a dairy cow's equipment is the udder, regardless of her breed.

He argued that the success of any dairy breed should be determined "by the ability of its cows to produce a profit at the milk pail and not by any competition at a fair." But fairs should attract the best available and honour the cows "that have already produced where it counts—back at the barn."

While working with Hays, I learned about the subtle but unmistakable division of farmers into social classes according to the breed of livestock a farmer specialized in. Hays told his audience of fellow breeders that any success he had enjoyed in their line of work was

because I never considered any animal—or any breed—from an aristocrat's point of view. I've always thought that all that really counts in the livestock business are the economics. It's not the social standing of an animal's breed, it's not its charm and grace and style that count most in any animal. It has to be how much of a profit it can produce, if any breeder intends to stay in business.

Hays had once driven 250 miles just to see Jane of Vernon, "the greatest Brown Swiss that ever lived." Many considered her one of the "best-uddered" cows of her day. Hays said: "I wanted to see what a best udder looked like so I'd know what to watch for next time." He had lingered in Toronto for two days in 1934 waiting for a chance to look at Brampton Basilua, the great Jersey champion. "And when you remember what Toronto used to be in those days, and that I'm from Calgary, you know how much I put up with." Two years later he had stayed over in Toronto for three days just to see the champion Ayrshire, Ardgowan Valdo. And in 1942 he had made a special trip to the Carnation farm near Seattle, Washington, "so that I could see for myself the champion Holstein, Carnation Ormsby Madcap Faine."

Hays dealt with these issues so bluntly and forcefully because he knew that there was strong opposition to his plan to reform the exhibition classifications. His assistant deputy minister Syd Williams remembered the meetings on Parliament Hill with the breed associations: "Jeeze, did they howl, particularly about the interbreed udder class. Nobody would judge it. Nobody would do anything. Now it's one of the most popular classes there are."

Hays later recalled the initial opposition to his package. After the announcement was made across Canada, "the feathers really hit the fan." Prime Minister Pearson began receiving hundreds of letters complaining that his minister of agriculture was ruining Canadian shows and exhibitions. Pearson was justifiably worried that Hays had lost hundreds of thousands of agricultural votes for the Liberal party. "Now let's take a look at the rewards," Hays said. "After fifteen years, for the most part the classification is still intact. I never go to a show but what at least a dozen times a day someone will comment how great the move was."

A text of Hays's "udders speech" was distributed among the Parliamentary Press Gallery, and reporters lost no time in drawing it to the attention of the Opposition. Most press gallery reporters found the speech amusing, but one who was not amused was Jean Charpentier of Ottawa's French-language newspaper, Le Droit. In a February 1965 column, he wrote: "When one feels reluctant to quote a minister of the Crown for fear of being accused of vulgar indecency, one starts to think that something has gone wrong. As nobody will take my word, I will take the risk of doing so, but not before apologizing first to the ladies who might read these lines."

Charpentier then quoted the udder references and continued:

Even for a Canadian minister of agriculture, there are boorish limits that such remarks obviously transgress. Nor is it the first time that Mr. Hays has expressed such grossness. At first it was taken as a particular style, but it has now become apparent that his insolent vulgarity is nothing but the expression of his equally insolent contempt for the public.

No politician can realistically expect to win them all, and not everyone agreed with everything Hays did or wanted to do. But Charpentier's does seem to be about the only truly bitter criticism levelled at Hays by the news media during his entire term as minister of agriculture.

Pearson had appointed the Royal Commission on Biculturalism and Bilingualism in July 1963 in response to the disturbances that separatists were causing in Quebec. The commission issued an interim report in 1965. Shortly afterwards, in a speech to the Edmonton West Liberal nomination convention, Hays expressed his views on the commission's preliminary findings. Wrote columnist Richard Jackson: "[Hays] became a Hill headliner when he put into proper perspective the great national 'crisis' that the Bilingual and Bicultural Commission so sensationally screamed it had discovered."

Hays had gauged the level of anti-French prejudice in Alberta and was well aware how skillfully Diefenbaker and some of his western followers were exploiting that prejudice whenever they were out of the national news media's hearing, and so he tried to deal with the touchy issue of unity between Canada's two founding races in the usual blunt-talking Hays style, hoping to make the words more acceptable to any Albertans listening in.

We seem to be living today in the age of the constant crisis. You just have to spend ten or fifteen minutes looking over a week's news, and you can start worrying over the crisis of your choice. We always seem to have at least fifty-seven varieties. . . . We have economic crises, labor crises, foreign exchange crises. Hardly a week goes by that I don't hear about some new agricultural crisis, and in Parliament we have a crisis a day and sometimes two or three.

Now we're told by the Royal Commission on Biculturalism and Bilingualism that we're in the middle of the worst crisis of national unity in our history. . . .

Personally, I can't get quite as worried as the B and B commissioners. And maybe they aren't as worried themselves as they have been made to sound in some of the news coverage of their preliminary report. . . . I found things in it that encourage me to think that our country is really on the threshold of a new era, a more exciting and rewarding era than any we've known in Canada before. . . .

My attention was drawn in particular to these words from the commission's French-language report: "More than most other countries, Canada is a creation of human will. It has been called a geographical absurdity, an appendage of the United States, a 4000-mile main street with many bare stretches. Nevertheless, this country has existed for a long time because its people have never stopped willing that there be a Canada."

To me the issue we face as a nation today is whether we are going to go on "willing that there be a Canada." I am absolutely confident that we are. . . . What I look forward to as the eventual outcome of this latest crisis [is] the rebirth of a richer and more dynamic Canada. Canadians are going to overcome this latest crisis, make no mistake about that. . . .

I believe as John F. Kennedy once said that our problems are man-made, and therefore they can be solved by man. We can be as big as we want, and it seems to me that the real challenge under all the others raised by our latest crisis of national unity is to every one of us to be maybe just a little bigger than we've ever been before.

Walter Stewart, in his 1965 Toronto *Star Weekly* profile, wrote that Hays's speeches were written mostly in folksy slang, and that when he inserted the occasional quotation of men like Robert Oppenheimer or Bernard Baruch, it "jars the ear; it's as if a hillbilly band suddenly broke into Beethoven." Hays began a speech to the Montreal Rotary Club in 1965 with this quip: "I still enjoy the way—when the wind's in the right direction in Montreal—you get whiffs of all that good, sound St. James street money. It takes me back to the stockyards in Calgary—where some of that money comes from." Under the headline "Fresh Breeze On Parliament Hill; Harry Hays Takes A No-Nonsense Approach," Calgary *Herald* reporter Jamie Portman described the speech as "a mixture of cracker barrel philosophy and political candor with a reference to the late French existentialist, Albert Camus, tossed in for good measure." (Once, when asked how he would respond if reporters inquired of him who Camus was, Hays replied: "I'll tell them he's the kind of thinker [Ottawa columnist and defeated New Democrat M.P.] Doug Fisher would like to be.")

The main theme of Hays's Montreal Rotary speech was a challenge to businessmen to couple with their legitimate criticisms of Big Government and its policies their suggestions for practical alternatives. He challenged business executives unhappy with government to enter the political arena and change things themselves.

Businessmen, he said, were always talking about how arbitrarily governments acted. "But in my short career as a cabinet minister," he bantered,

I haven't come across anybody in government—or even in the Opposition or the press gallery—as arbitrary, as opinionated or as downright dictatorial as some of the bank managers and company presidents I have known. If businessmen and other assorted tycoons are unhappy with the government, then let them leave their teakpanelled board rooms, or come back from their extended spring vacations, and take some direct personal action to make our governments work the way they think they should.

He could think of quite a few of his business executive acquaintances whom he would love to see in a federal cabinet post for a few years where they would have to answer to the whole country for every decision they made.

Some of these rather pious and condescending critics of government from the business world think it's almost an unbearable nuisance just to have to spend one day a year accounting for their actions to a few stockholders. I wonder how much of their executive infallibility would survive if they had to win majority support from a stockholders' meeting for every major decision they take before putting it into practice.

If the glare of public scrutiny were ever directed into the inner sanctums of business enterprises, Hays had a strong suspicion that the executives would be revealed to be just as prone to error in running their businesses as cabinet ministers were in running the country. "I mention these things with all due respect and modesty and tact," Hays said, tongue firmly in cheek, "only to emphasize my point that it isn't [big] organizations that we need to worry about. It is the calibre and leadership capacities of the people running the organizations."

This speech, too, attracted considerable news media attention. (One parliamentary correspondent, on reading a transcript of the speech, said that there was nothing in it worth filing to his paper. "But," he added, "wasn't it delightful reading?")

The day after his Montreal speech, Hays was back in Ottawa to face, along with three cabinet colleagues, Mitchell Sharp, Roger Teillet and Maurice Sauvé, a delegation of twelve hundred unhappy Ontario Farmers' Union members. They were demanding higher incomes, especially through increases in federal support payments for various farm products raised in their province.

Just as Hays was about to start speaking to the angry group, his executive assistant, Don McIntosh, hurried to his side. He had intercepted one of several notes being circulated among the delegates urging them not to applaud Hays and to boo him when their leaders did. Hays forced a grin, drew attention to the note in his hand and told his audience that it would make no difference to his concern about legitimate farm problems.

He assured the farmers that he was on their side. He knew farmers had many problems, in eastern as in western Canada. The government was developing policies that would ensure farmers a minimum annual income of about $4,500—at that time the average annual industrial wage. (In August 1984 the average annual industrial wage stood at $20,974; the average family income was about $32,000 per year.)

Then Hays turned to the seventeen-page submission to cabinet prepared by the Ontario Farmers' Union executive and, unfazed by jeers and catcalls, pointed out the serious errors with which he believed it was riddled. In particular, he rejected as economically unworkable farm price supports made on a regional basis. As he had stressed from the beginning of his ministry, farm problems had to be solved on a national basis. The result of regional price supports would be subsidized uneconomic production in some areas competing unfairly with unsubsidized economic production in other areas (a condition widespread in Canada twenty years later because of a proliferation of provincial farm subsidy programs using tax funds to compete among each other for markets.)

The farmers, after being told by Hays that many of their demands were unrealistic and unworkable, marched out angrier than when they had arrived. They picked up their placards and went protesting on Parliament Hill. The next day in the Commons, Hays calmly responded to Opposition questions about the troublesome meeting by stating that he expected the Pearson government, before it was through, to do more for farmers than any other government had done.

This was not the only time Hays's personal knowledge about farming caused annoyance within farm organizations. "Sometimes," one of his officials recalled, "they were offended by his use of his own knowledge to shoot down their suggestions." Farm organization leaders quickly learned that it was pointless trying to put any carelessly thought-out proposals past Hays.

Common sense and frankness characterized Hays's entire career. Those present at his first private meeting with executives of the Canadian Federation of Agriculture remembered long afterward how impatient he had become over the drawn-out presentation. The president, Jim Bentley, started out reading the formal, written volume. When after some time his voice gave out, he called upon the executive manager, Dave Kirk, to finish the reading. All the while, Hays kept hitching forward impatiently in his chair and drumming his fingers on the table. When at last Kirk finished, Hays looked from him to Bentley, tried to chuckle good-naturedly and said: "You sure as hell gave us the whole bundle in one forkful, didn't you?"

Assessing Hays, the Calgary *Herald*'s Jamie Portman wrote:

The frankness of many of his public utterances often leaves his more fervent admirers clutching their heads in despair. But there seems to be a growing consensus that, whatever Mr. Hays may lack in diplomacy or delicacy, it is downright hazardous to try and fault him in his capacity for work or in his grasp of the multifaceted operations of his vast department. Mr. Hays emerges as the plain, blunt, no-nonsense man of the cabinet, thundering in where his more discreet colleagues fear to tread. . . .

Observers considered Mr. Hays's meeting with the farmers to be a fascinating display, a typical Haysian performance. "How does he get away with it?" was one admiring comment.

That Hays did get away with this approach perhaps explains why his presence on the Hill was so often greeted with such a mingling of wrath, admiration and delighted incredulity.

CHAPTER TWELVE

HIS
OWN
NICHE

B y the spring of 1965, only two years after
being elected to the House of Commons and named minister of agriculture, Harry Hays was carving a niche of his own in national politics, and he could list a growing array of his own farm policies,
claims like Peter Newman's on this issue in *The Distemper of Our
Times* to the contrary notwithstanding. And by the time Prime Minister Pearson, in a desperate attempt to turn his embattled government's minority into a majority, called a federal election for 8 November, Hays's policy list was measurably longer.

Newman in his 1968 book dismissed the Pearson government's
agricultural platform for the 1965 election as "meaningless rhetoric"
and "an open-ended subsidy program" applying only to western
grain and a few sheep. In fact, the platform was extensive enough

to fill a four-page tabloid distributed nationally from Liberal party headquarters in Ottawa. And several planks were unique in Canadian farm policy up to that time.

Hays summarized his farm policy plans in a private five-page letter which Prime Minister Pearson had requested as part of that fall's preparation for the election campaign; the material in it was intended for use in campaign literature. Hays wrote that the government's agriculture program for the election would complete the program already begun for farmers in all parts of Canada. Hays rejected the hand-out approach because it provided no lasting solutions to farm problems. The government's program was based on realistic economic principles designed to reduce farmers' reliance on government aid and to build up their independence and self-sufficiency. The program had three primary points: adequate credit at reasonable interest rates; a minimum income security through crop insurance and price stabilization, and more bargaining power for producers in the marketing of their products. Hays had already doubled the credit available to farmers and had made crop insurance more workable; price stabilization mechanisms are still evolving.

His main goal, he stated, continued to be a minimum average annual net income for the family farm equivalent to the national average industrial wage. He wrote: "This is as precise a definition of a parity farm income as has yet been produced by any party." This definition may still hold today. In Quebec a similar link to wage-earners' incomes is used in determining provincial farm price subsidies.

Measures by which Hays's goal would be pursued included, first, further revisions to the crop insurance program to make it available to every Canadian farmer within eighteen months (in 1985 it paid millions to prairie farmers who would otherwise have been ruined by drought), and second, establishment of the already planned Canadian Dairy Commission as the forerunner of similar national marketing systems for other farm products to be established in consultation with the provinces, to allow producers greater control over marketing. (The Dairy Commission still operates successfully, and has been joined by the Grain Commission, the Livestock Feed Board, the Farm Products Marketing Council and the Freshwater

Fish Marketing Board. (The Canadian Wheat Board was established in 1935.)

Hays listed a total of sixteen planks in his platform. These did not include achievements already in place, such as a $650,000 contribution towards the construction of the first Canadian veterinary college of this century, and the first ever in western Canada, at the University of Saskatchewan in Saskatoon.

Unemployment insurance and workmen's compensation coverage for farm workers were poorly received, especially by farmers, who were unenthusiastic about the programs' complex record-keeping requirements. Much of the rest of Hays's program became academic with his defeat. Nevertheless, it was a very respectable farm program for any government at any time.

Hays's biggest immediate challenge when he became agriculture minister had been what to do about a Diefenbaker government dairy subsidy program that Alvin Hamilton had let slide out of control. Syd Williams, who later served as deputy minister of agriculture and on retirement was Hays's partner in a Calgary-based farm consulting operation, was chairman of the Agricultural Stabilization Board when Hays first arrived in his new job. He thought what made Hays unique among agriculture ministers, at least until then, was his knowledge about agriculture from personal experience; as a consequence, Hays knew what farmers needed.

Williams recalled how quickly Hays brought the program under control. When Hays became minister, the Stabilization Board had huge surpluses of products, butter in particular, and for a long time it could not prompt the Diefenbaker government to deal with these stockpiles. Hays promptly asked Williams for advice.

Williams told him that the first thing they should do was put a stop to government buying. In providing support for farm product prices from then on, the government should rely on a system of deficiency payments—subsidies to make up the difference between market price and what was considered a fair return for the producers. Hays told Williams: "Get out and sell the damn stuff. The first loss is the least loss." There were approximately 330 million pounds of butter on hand then. All of it was sold. Williams said: "I went all over the world, practically, selling the damn stuff. We sold a lot of it in Canada, too. We increased per capita consumption from fourteen to eighteen pounds."

Early in his ministerial days, Hays had concluded that two sets of farm policies were needed, "one set for the farmers who are economic, or potentially economic, operators and another set for the farmers who are not." The farmer on poor land that would never earn him a living was "more of a welfare than an agricultural problem." The farmer who posed an agricultural policy problem—"one," Hays said, "which I believe can be solved"—was the one who was not earning a decent living, simply because he had not expanded his operation to an economically viable size.

One of the first things Hays had done to facilitate farm expansion and consolidation was to introduce legislation that generously increased the credit available to farmers from the federal Farm Credit Corporation. It now could lend up to 75 per cent of a farm's appraised value to a maximum of $40,000 for a standard mortgage loan, and to $55,000 for a supervised package loan secured at least 60 per cent by land and buildings and not more than 40 per cent by livestock and equipment. These are small amounts by today's inflated standards, but they were substantial at that time—twice what they had been under the Diefenbaker regime.

Hays left the repayment period for the standard mortgage loan at thirty years, where the Tories had set it. But with typical attention to the helpful detail, he revised the repayment provisions for the packaged loans. The Tories had legislated that the 40 per cent covered by livestock and equipment had to be repaid over the first ten years. Hays legislated that the whole package loan be repaid over the full thirty-year period. He explained why this would be especially helpful to a young farmer just starting out: Previously, if he borrowed $16,000, he had to repay $1,380 a year for the first nine years and $770 a year over the remainder of the thirty-year period. "His biggest payments were in the years when usually he'd have his hardest going, at the beginning." His change, Hays pointed out, meant "he would pay $1,056 a year for the full period, which works out to $324 a year less during his first nine years."

To make it easier for family farms to remain in the family, Hays introduced two other small-print changes with life-sized impact. One enabled a farmer to borrow on his farm's equity to expand his own farm, to help a son, daughter or other close relative buy a new farm, or to finance handing down the farm to the next generation when the farmer retired. The other provided that a loan could be made to a deceased farmer's executor or administrator to permit heirs to continue farming their family farm even if they were too young to qualify for the loan. The loan would revert to the heirs when they came of age.

Hays could also claim much success in his handling of dairy industry problems, beginning virtually within hours of his entering office, with helpful advice from Syd Williams and Deputy Minister Cliff Barry. His first one-year dairy program, running from 1 May 1963 to 30 April 1964, had been intended to divert milk from production of butter and skim milk powder into production of cheese. Cheddar cheese production that dairy year had risen to 137.2 million pounds from 116.6 million the year before. Less than two years later, by early 1965, he could also report that the huge butter surplus of 1963 had been liquidated.

In May 1964, at the beginning of his second one-year dairy program, Hays had aimed at an even more precise cheese target by subtly changing the basis for the government's deficiency payment from 30 cents per hundredweight of milk to 3.6 cents per pound of first-grade cheddar. He did this because first-grade cheese could be sold in export markets as production exceeded demand at home, whereas surplus lower graded cheeses could not be and so could easily disrupt the market. By November 1964 first-grade cheddar accounted for 94.6 per cent of all cheese produced in Canada, up from 87.3 per cent in 1963.

Speaking in the Commons on 13 April—only nine days short of his second anniversary as minister of agriculture—Hays was in a position to hammer the Tories hard over their dairy and other agriculture policies. And he did.

> Their stock-in-trade was the hand-out approach. They lacked either the imagination or the guts to bring in solid and responsible policies aimed at providing lasting solutions to our agricultural problems. What they apparently wanted most from all their policies were votes. They didn't care how much of the taxpayers' money they had to spend trying to buy them or how much they worsened the long-term problems of agriculture in the process.

"The mess they made of the dairy program is a good example,"

he said. The Tories had been "too chicken-hearted" to put dairy
returns on a sound basis—"a basis that would not eventually have
wrecked the industry with an ever-increasing surplus of production." Hays's dairy program was designed to bring about a return
for manufacturing milk which, on a national average basis, would be
equal to $3.50 per hundredweight—compared with $2.80 to $3.00
up to a year previous. It was also designed to discourage production that exceeded Canada's domestic needs.

> In crop insurance it was the same story. [The Tories] brought in a
> program our farmers need, but it was . . . left to this government to
> straighten it out and make it work. They brought in the ARDA [Agri-
> cultural Rehabilitation and Development Act] program and then made
> such a mess of the whole country's finances that they couldn't afford
> to get it off the ground. It wasn't until this government took over and
> straightened out their financial mess that ARDA really got rolling.
> They expanded farm credit, but again they only went half far enough.

With remarkable speed and comprehension, Hays had been able
to grasp the whole position of agriculture within the Canadian
economy. He had swiftly appreciated the complex reasons, for example, why the price for drinking milk had risen over the previous
ten years from $2.37 per hundredweight to $4.79, while the manufacturing-milk price had only risen from $2.52 to $2.67. Surplus
drinking milk could be diverted to the manufacturing market for
production of butter, cheese and powder, to depress manufacturing-milk prices instead of drinking-milk prices. This was why
Hays was now working so hard to establish a national milk marketing system that clearly separated the operations of the dairy industry's two very different sectors.

He could point out as well that "price alone cannot correct the
economic difficulties of the numerous small producers." The Agricultural Stabilization Board had estimated that more than 40 per
cent of all manufacturing-milk producers in Canada delivered an annual average of only 22,176 pounds of milk. Even an increase of 50
cents per hundredweight would increase their income by just under
$10 a month. It was further estimated that at least half the
manufacturing-milk producers were operating units too small to
achieve a satisfactory economic position on milk alone. "This dif-

ficulty," Hays said, "can be corrected only by the enlargement of the smaller units"—one of the reasons for his farm credit amendments.

Something Alvin Hamilton had said in October 1963, when Hays faced the Commons for the first time in defence of his departmental spending estimates, had bothered him off and on ever since. He finally got it off his chest at an Ottawa news conference in January 1965. But Diefenbaker so distorted Hays's message that a month later Hays had to explain what he had really said, both in the Commons and to fellow Liberal M.P.s.

What "stuck in my craw," Hays said, was Hamilton's reference to a set of figures which he had said indicated that 25 per cent of the farmers across Canada earned less than $1,200 from their farms. At the news conference, Hays had said that he could not accept those figures as accurate, whatever their source.

"I was not suggesting," he explained in a letter to Quebec M.P. Hermann Laverdière,

> that $1,200 a year or $2,400 a year in gross income is anywhere near enough for any farmer to live on decently. I was only arguing that any farmer with two hogs and six cows had a potential gross income of more than $2,400 a year, whatever economists and politicians more at home in ivory towers than barnyards might argue to the contrary.
>
> If a farmer has two sows, they would each have two litters of pigs a year, and if they just made the national average of eight pigs per litter, that would come to 32 pigs in a year. If they were sold on the Montreal market when they were five or six months old and weighed about 200 pounds, they would bring something like $40 apiece. That is a gross income of $1,280, and he still has the two sows.
>
> If, in addition to the two sows, he has six cows, each giving the national average of 8000 pounds of milk per year, that is 48,000 pounds of milk. At the current Quebec price of $3.20 per hundredweight, that is a gross income of $1,536, although figuring it in my head at the news conference I just used a round figure of "over $1,200." So if you add the hog gross of $1,280 to the milk gross of $1,536 you get a total gross income of $2,816 for a farmer with two sows and six cows.
>
> My contention at the news conference was that anybody who

doesn't have a couple of pigs and half a dozen cows around his place just shouldn't consider himself a farmer, and that kind of rural dweller should not be included in statistics intended to give an accurate picture of our farm problems.

Months after Hays had put his explanation on the Hansard record, Diefenbaker was still misquoting him. " 'If a Quebec farmer had two sows, six cows and a wife with a strong back, he can make $2,400 a year.' You wouldn't believe it unless you read it in Hansard. Here it is . . . page 11580," he would claim as though he were indeed quoting from that page. But Hays had never made any reference in the Commons to a "wife with a strong back"; that was pure Diefenbakerian invention. What Hays had joked at his news conference was that if such a farmer's wife "got rid of her husband, she'd be better off," because then she might at least qualify for welfare.

By the time of his Tory-hammering Commons speech in April 1965, Hays could point out that he had now studied at first hand the agricultural policies and farm problems of ten other countries to see what he might apply to new policies in Canada. He had added to his Russian and European visits a journey to New Zealand and Australia, and he had been to Washington as well. He announced to the Commons that Canada was behind most of those other countries "in establishing policies that [would] ensure a strong, economically sound food production industry."

Canada, his travelling study exercises had convinced him, was furthest behind in establishing a comprehensive national policy to cover the entire agricultural economy. Hays did not believe that any solution was to be found with hand-outs or subsidy programs that only encouraged unhealthy surpluses. He accused the Tories of having taken an ad hoc approach to agricultural problems for too long. Now his government intended to develop, in co-operation with the provinces, a national agricultural program based on economic principles which as far as possible could be placed beyond the reach of political expediencies.

This program must ensure a stable supply of food for our consumers at reasonable prices. It must recognize the legitimate interests in our domestic market of our trading partners. But it must

also recognize the right of every farmer in this country to an income
that is more closely equivalent to what the workers in our towns and
cities enjoy. We now have labour laws guaranteeing minimum wages
for our workers. We have tariffs and tax incentives for our businessmen. It's time we started thinking of a minimum income for our
farmers.

This was a unique basis for a national agricultural policy. The
challenge, as Hays tried to develop this idea into practical political
policy, had been how such a minimum farm income could fairly be
determined. Hays presented his solution:

In 1949 the average weekly industrial wage was equivalent to
$2,236 per year. In the same year the average realized net income of
farmers was almost the same, $2,283. In 1964, however, the
average industrial wage had increased to $4,472 while the average
farm income was only $3,815—a difference of nearly $700. I believe
the primary objective of all our agricultural programs should be to encourage a [minimum] national average realized net income for the
family farm, equivalent to the national average industrial wage.

This, Hays concluded, should be the definition for policy purposes
of the minimum income starting point for "an economic family farm
unit."

In presenting to Parliament his new idea that a minimum income
should be the foundation for national farm policy, Hays could not
resist another run at Hamilton, Diefenbaker and his other critics.

They still think of the family farm as a few acres of badly cultivated
land, six tired cows, a couple of worn-out sows, book-keeping on the
back of an envelope, a shed or two, a tarpaper shack, a mail-order
catalogue and an outhouse. That's not a family farm. That's a welfare
problem. And we have policies for that, too.

He also used the occasion to repeat a suggestion he had already
been making outside Parliament—that Canada might take a page
from other countries' policies for putting more farmers on economic
units. He said the federal and provincial governments might soon
consider establishing a comprehensive national program for pur-

chasing poorly used lands and developing them into economic family farm units. The units would be sold or leased back to farmers who could then be expected to earn a decent living on them.

Hays said everything that the Pearson government had done in farm programs to date had been geared towards establishing a national agriculture policy keyed to the viable family farm. The next step, he said, was to develop policies that would assure Canadian farmers the level of markets and incomes that would enable them to pay for the intended expansion.

His broad hint of wanting to establish a national farm marketing system, with farmers having more say in their prices than ever before, was not missed by everyone in the news media. The *Financial Times of Canada* in May 1965 reported: "The seeds of a new and radically different federal agricultural policy have been planted by the government. The policy involves easing up on direct government support for products and spending more on the farms themselves."

Roy Atkinson, president of the Saskatchewan Farmers' Union in Saskatoon, had been paying attention to what Hays had been saying publicly even before his Commons statement. Atkinson told the *Star-Phoenix* that if a national agricultural policy adjusted to maintain economic farm units were to be established as Hays was advocating, "it could mean a major breakthrough towards farm advancement." It would be the first time an effort had been made to establish an example of an economic farm unit. Farmers would have a definite standard to work towards in organizing their own farm operations.

One opponent of Hays's new farm policy was his home-town ally, the right-wing Calgary *Herald.* If Hays's "rather fancy goals" were to be achieved, it editorialized, "it will only be through federal farm aid and planning on a greater scale than this country has ever known in the past, and could represent a sharp break with the free-enterprise tradition which has governed farming operations up until now." Measuring farm income against the wages of industry "appears to be heading in the direction of farm-union and NDP policies of Socialistic state planning. It assumes that the family farm unit is an economic asset as such and ignores the role which the ability of each individual farmer to manage a farm unit capably must play."

Hays disputed this. He argued that the deficiency payment system of support left a very important area in which the producer's own private enterprise remained an essential factor; in the case of a dairy farmer, that area lay in his dealings with the processing plant. Hays used his latest dairy program to illustrate his point. The program did not provide a guarantee to each producer, but rather to the industry as a whole. "It does not mean that every shipper will receive exactly $3.50. The farmer's total return will still depend on how well he does in negotiating the price he gets at the plant."

Hays pointed out that if the deficiency payment were to be, say, 25 cents per hundredweight, and a farmer managed to get $3.10 from the plant, this plus the supplementary payment of 20 cents would give him a total return of $3.55 per hundredweight, whereas the farmer who settled for only $3.00 from his plant would end up receiving only $3.45.

Hays revealed his reason for stressing the role of producer enterprise in negotiating a milk price with the processor. "We have heard that some producers are being persuaded to accept lower plant prices with the argument that they don't have to worry, the government will make up for the lower plant price." That, Hays said, was false. As far as he was concerned, free enterprise in Canada's farm community was still far from dead. Let the seller—as well as the buyer—beware.

Hays appreciated the extent to which a farmer's personal enterprise in improving efficiency, regardless of government policies, could raise his farm's income. "We could produce another $100 to $200 million worth of produce from exactly the same farms and land now in production by paying more attention to this question of efficiency." The average Canadian hog required approximately three pounds of feed to produce a pound of pork, whereas in Denmark, efficiency had cut this down to 2.1 for 1, a difference of $4 per hog, or nearly $30 million for all hogs then produced in Canada. Or, an increase of ten bushels per acre in barley production by growing only the most productive varieties would mean another $30 to $40 million earned from the same acreage. Or, an increase of only two bushels per acre in wheat yields would be worth another $100 million from the same acreage.

Hays's relatively radical proposals did alarm some of his civil service advisers and startle his cabinet colleagues. In the Commons he had once said: "If these sound like radical approaches, I defend them by pointing out that our problems are radical." The *Globe* magazine in early 1965 commented: "When they catch up with their member's thinking back in Calgary South, some of the Tories and Socreds are going to wonder if they elected a right-wing Liberal or a left-wing New Democrat."

Back in his home province of Alberta, too, Hays had been getting some flak, mostly in private, from Liberals who did not support all of his farm policy ideas. Nor did they like his refusal to shift over to Liberals his ministry's patronage jobs and contracts that had been awarded by the Diefenbaker Tories. His attitude towards this legitimate patronage was no doubt a mistake in political tactics. And it was a mistake that the Tories, still feeding from this particular public trough, often chuckled about, out of Hays's hearing, but in the presence of Liberals envious of jobs and contracts they had assumed the change of government would automatically have switched to them. "I am not interested," Hays once told a group of Liberals, "in the patronage or expedient approach on any of our national problems, including the problems of agriculture." Understandably, such Liberals smarted at Hays's steadfast—and unquestionably naive—antipatronage stand.

In the spring of 1965 Hays presented a written response to the highly critical "conclusions and recommendations recently arrived at by the Alberta Agricultural Committee," a Liberal body. One of their complaints was that Hays was not doing enough to help "the family farm." Romanticism more than realism seemed to have inspired these complaints. The Liberal critics in Alberta were asking for policies to subsidize smaller acreages as though their very smallness gave them an inherent social or moral superiority over larger acreages. The family farm was precisely what Hays was trying to preserve, but he knew that the family farm had to be big enough before it could be profitable. Another of their main objections was that the two-price wheat policy promised by Hazen Argue on behalf of the Pearson government during the 1963 election campaign was not being implemented.

On the family farm issue, Hays responded: "Our whole agricultural program is oriented to the family farm. But let's remember that the family farm has changed." He again used the case of the two-sow, six-cow farm and pointed out that that was a welfare problem, easily tackled through ARDA and other redevelopment programs.

The issue of two-price wheat (an issue that surfaced again in late 1984 when Canadian Wheat Board President Charles Mayer suggested that the domestic price of wheat be doubled) Hays dismissed out of hand as unworkable and not even that beneficial to wheat farmers. Explained Hays:

> We couldn't have a two-price system for our exports without seriously undermining the unexcelled position in world markets of the Wheat Board. American wheat farmers get subsidies. But they also must operate under strict quotas to qualify. Are those who advocate government subsidies for wheat ready to accept production controls along with them? I don't think so. The two-price system was promised during the last election campaign. The voting on the prairies indicated what most farmers thought of that promise.

A two-price system could not even be applied to wheat used within Canada for animal feed purposes. Setting a higher price for this wheat at home than could be obtained on world markets would cause Canadian farmers to switch to less costly substitutes, such as U.S. corn. Since wheat used in domestic consumption averaged only 10 per cent of normal total marketings, an increase of 50 cents a bushel on domestic wheat would amount to only about 6.5 cents per bushel spread over total marketings. "This would have to be covered by a consumer subsidy, or bread would go up 2 cents a loaf or more," Hays said. "Even then, this kind of subsidy would go mostly to a relatively few large producers, the people who need help least."

When Hays reviewed his policies for Pearson as the government geared up for the autumn election, he also referred to two others soon to be realized.

> Agreement has been reached with France and the United States for the importation into Canada, for the first time, of French Charolais beef cattle. Many Canadian breeders believe this will lead to an eventual, and substantial, improvement in the efficiency of beef production in Canada. France has agreed, for the first time, to permit

importation of Canadian Holstein cattle. To promote as many sales as possible in this market, my department is launching on September 1st a travelling exhibit of 20 of these cattle throughout rural France over the following two months.

Behind those few sentences of information for the prime minister lay many weeks of difficult and delicate negotiations that presaged some lasting changes to the nature of the North American beef industry.

CHAPTER THIRTEEN

THE CHAROLAIS CAPER

On a livestock exporting trip to Mexico and Cuba in 1945, Harry Hays encountered what he described as "the best cattle I had ever seen." They were French Charolais crossbreeds. Immediately, he thought of buying some to take home for breeding purposes. But he learned that because of animal health regulations in Canada and the United States, it was impossible to import Charolais at that time.

Foot-and-mouth disease had long been a farm plague in Europe, where vaccination was one way of fighting it. Canada and the United States had managed to remain virtually free of the disease, however, so both followed a policy of allowing no cattle imports from countries where any cattle had had the disease or had been vaccinated against it. In any rare instance when the disease might appear in Canada or the United States, the policy was the same on both sides of the border: all animals in an infected herd must be slaughtered immediately and their carcasses burned.

But Hays never forgot the Charolais, and when he became minister of agriculture, he decided to arrange for their importation from France, even though the same animal health regulations still prevailed in North America.

Hays knew that although he was now in a position to change Canadian farm policies, including the prohibitions that prevented the importation of Charolais, he could not do so without the approval of the U.S. secretary of agriculture. There was virtually an open border for cattle sales between Canada and the United States. Canada sold more cattle to the United States than to any other country. But if a single animal were imported into Canada against U.S. animal health regulations, that border could be closed instantly, with enormous economic harm to Canadian cattle producers.

One of the first moves Hays made was to assign Canadian Veterinary General Dr. Ken Wells to develop a proposal for allowing Canadian breeders to import Charolais cattle in a way that would pose no health risk in Canada and would be acceptable to the United States. Above all, there must be no possibility whatsoever that the United States might suddenly close its border to Canadian cattle sales because of an imported Charolais.

Hays's next step was to find opportunities to discuss the idea informally with Orville Freeman, the U.S. agriculture secretary. The periodic meetings, alternating between Washington and Ottawa, of the consultative committee of Canadian and American cabinet ministers, soon provided this chance. During one of the committee's Ottawa sessions, Hays arranged a small private dinner for Freeman in the New Zealand Room, adjoining the Parliamentary restaurant.

There, after a pleasantly drawn-out dinner lashed with liberal servings of French wine, Freeman agreed to direct the animal health officials in his department to work with Wells and his officials in Hays's department to produce a plan for importing the Charolais into Canada on terms acceptable to the United States. Several months of negotiations between the two capitals finally produced a deal acceptable both to Wells and the U.S. officials. It only remained for Hays to obtain final confirmation of the plan's acceptability from Freeman. His method of accomplishing this indicated how perceptive he was of the nuances of human behaviour.

Instead of asking pointblank for Freeman's approval, a move that would have forced Freeman to take personal responsibility for approving the agreement, Hays simply telephoned the agriculture secretary in Washington and advised him that, on the basis of the agreement reached by their officials, he now planned to go ahead with the first importations of Charolais. In this way, Hays freed him from taking such direct responsibility for the decision. He made it as easy as possible for Freeman to indicate his tacit approval. Freeman need not even say he approved the agreement. He need only not raise any objection, and Hays could feel free to proceed.

Freeman listened carefully. He neither orally approved the agreement nor raised any objection to Hays going ahead with his planned Charolais importations. It went as Hays had hoped, and within a few weeks he was ready to fly to France to complete arrangements with the French Charolais breeders' organization.

Hays spelled out the stringent importation precautions negotiated with the French in a May speech to the British Columbia Beef Growers' Association. His thoroughness reflected his awareness that not every breeder in Canada was happy about this new competition soon to arrive from France. One of the most vociferous opponents was an Aberdeen Angus breeder and friend from the Calgary area, Donald Matthews, who organized a group of petitioners to oppose Hays's plan right up to Prime Minister Pearson. Although Pearson had given him the go-ahead, Hays was still anxious to encourage all the support he could muster.

He told the Beef Growers' Association that although health regulations to prevent foot-and-mouth disease were necessary, they should not be applied to the point of restricting imports of bloodlines which might be useful to the Canadian livestock industry. He pointed out that English cattle had suffered periodic outbreaks of the disease; it was controlled there as in Canada by slaughtering infected herds. Yet Canada had for years been importing English cattle, provided they went through a quarantine station in Scotland, historically free of the disease. U.S. animal health laws prevented direct importation of English cattle, but for years many American breeders had been importing British cattle by first bringing them into Canada. Hays now proposed to do the same with cattle from France.

He stressed that any cattle Canada imported must come from areas in which there had been no foot-and-mouth outbreaks. Only unvaccinated calves would be imported. Animals would be disease-tested while still on the French owners' premises. The calves would be transported via disease-free routes to a quarantine station at Brest, on the northwest coast, where they would be further tested. After thirty days they would be shipped to the security quarantine station of the Canadian agriculture department on Gros Isle, a former immigrant quarantine station in the St. Lawrence River downstream from Quebec City, where they would be tested yet again. As further insurance, all the blood samples from Gros Isle were to be sent to the world's most experienced research centre in the disease at Pirbright, England, for final testing. Canadian regulations required that the animals be kept there a minimum of ninety days, but in fact it would be closer to five months because they would arrive just before the river froze in late fall and would be unable to leave until the river broke up in spring.

The length to which Hays and his animal health experts had gone to ensure that there was absolutely no danger in the program was evident from the fact that the incubation period for foot-and-mouth disease is only seven days.

Unfortunately for some breeders, the Gros Isle quarantine station could handle only 124 head of cattle at one time. Those places would soon be filled by animals purchased by sixty-seven Canadian breeders who had successfully qualified for import permits. (Hays used to tell the amusing story of how his department had only two vehicles on Gros Isle, where there was no more than a mile of road in total, and one day they managed to have a head-on collision.)

Hays had also insisted on stringent performance potential in any of the Charolais sold to Canadian breeders. The unvaccinated calves had to have weighed 100 pounds at birth and have gained 100 pounds per month during their first six months. They must also have come from a mother that weighed between 1800 and 2000 pounds and a sire that weighed closer to 3000 pounds. Hays said: "Anyone the least bit familiar with livestock will see right away from these standards why breeders in Canada—and the United States—are so interested in these animals."

□   □   □

Hays, Deputy Minister Cliff Barry, his assistant Syd Williams and I flew overnight from Montreal to Paris, where a trade commissioner, our companion and guide, joined us. The trade commissioner had his own automobile, and the Hays party travelled in a Cadillac limousine. Our destination was Navarre in the luscious Loire River valley, a countryside of rolling fields and rounded hills with patches of forest on them and lavish, ancient wine chateaus.

A light on the limousine's dashboard indicated that the generator was not working. Our chauffeur smiled brightly and said it was always on when the motor was running; that was how he knew the generator *was* working.

An hour or so from the airport, we arrived at the first of several Charolais farms to be visited that weekend and, with our high-spirited hosts, began our memorable trip across the beautiful French countryside. At several of the farms, we came upon Canadian breeders who were already picking out the calves they wanted to import that October. As the day wore spiritedly on, we noticed that our chauffeur kept the engine running during our stops.

The French farmers we visited, all of whom seemed well-to-do and some wealthy, entertained us in their homes and made us feel warmly welcome. And for good reason.

Until he initiated negotiations with French Agriculture Minister Edgard Pisani and the Charolais breeders, Hays later told Calgary *Herald* farm writer John Schmidt,

> the French didn't realize what a valuable property they had on their hands. They were going to smaller beef cattle as we were with the British breeds. However, they had retained the Charolais as draft animals for farm work, although their days were numbered as farm mechanization spread. They would no doubt have disappeared had we not shown an interest in them as genetic material.

One of our stops was at what was supposed to be a temporary quarantine station for calves waiting to be shipped in a group to Brest. Hays, Williams and Barry took a long, silent look at the single strand of barbed wire surrounding the holding area. They were afraid to look at each other for fear of laughing. Hays politely suggested to his hosts that perhaps a few more strands of wire would make the area more secure.

At another stop, our hosts were about to present a gift Charolais calf, a fine-looking prize animal, to Hays as a free and sincere token of their appreciation for what he was doing to revive such wide international interest in their breed. Hays thanked them profusely for their generous intentions and, occasionally gazing longingly at the calf, explained as tactfully as possible, as his hosts' expressions turned momentarily to disappointment, that he could not accept such a gift because it would be considered improper political behaviour back in Canada and would cause him embarrassment. Afterward he said she was the best-looking calf he had seen on the whole trip.

Our journey ended with a long late-afternoon banquet, with many courses, much wine and a variety of happy toasts, in an ancient hotel in Navarre, reputedly a favourite of Napoleon's. We slept there that night and awoke the next morning to learn from our worried chauffeur that his battery was *"mort."* It was Sunday, and we were due in Paris that evening. From somewhere, however, the chauffeur managed to produce a Peugeot for our return journey.

As a spinoff of his Charolais deal, Hays also negotiated a foot in the door through France to the European market for Canadian Holstein dairy cattle. Hays had frequently expressed an interest in getting Canadian cattle into the European market, and he thought that France was the place to try. Importation was then controlled in France by the breed associations. Hays decided that the way to work around that was to persuade the users of the cattle—not the purebred breeders but the fellows who were actually milking cows out in the country—that Canadian Holsteins had something to offer.

With this in mind, he negotiated with Agriculture Minister Pisani permission to send to France a herd of Holsteins to exhibit in several rural communities, so that farmers could see for themselves what the Canadian animals could produce. This was only a part of Hays's challenge, however. His biggest battle was against the bureaucrats in the Canadian trade and commerce department. By rights, they should have been the ones organizing a travelling livestock herd. They refused to do it, evidently not appreciating the potential that Hays saw for new sales of Canadian cattle abroad. And they did not want the agriculture department to organize it, either.

Eventually there was quite a serious fight over the matter in

cabinet. Mitchell Sharp, following the advice of his trade and commerce officials, said that his department would not spend money on
the exhibition. His officials did not believe such a complicated project could be carried out successfully. So Hays persuaded Treasury
Board to approve the money for his own department to do it. He
then recruited veteran livestock showman R. O. ("Dick") Biggs, an
acquaintance from his livestock exhibiting days, to put together the
herd and show it around France.

Although the project proved enormously challenging, Biggs, a
shy, quiet man, persevered, and finally, on 12 August 1965, the
aircraft carrying the twenty head of high-performing Holsteins arrived in France. But not without adventure.

The plane had been fully loaded a few days earlier, the two bulls,
five two-year-old heifers and thirteen cows had all been sedated for
the trans-Atlantic flight, and the engines were warming up for takeoff when the pilot walked back through the aircraft for one final
check on the animals. As he looked into the space where a bull was
bedded down, the animal suddenly tossed its head, one of its horns
slashing the pilot's forehead. The plane had to taxi back to its loading ramp, the engines were shut down, and the pilot was rushed to
hospital, where he received several stitches. The animals were un-
loaded and were returned to their pens. When the pilot was fit to
fly again, and the flight had been rescheduled, Biggs reloaded his
cattle and resedated them. This time the plane took off safely. But
over the Atlantic it ran into very high winds and was tossed about
quite wildly. The plane had to land in Iceland and again in Ireland to
ensure that the animals were able to remain secure in their places.
Finally they arrived, as shaken as Biggs by the turbulent flight, at
the quarantine station at Le Touquet.

The old showman had just a little more than two weeks to get
the animals into exhibition shape. The herd was scheduled to go on
public display on 1 September in the northern French farming community of Amiens. Hays had fitted into a very tight schedule a
twenty-four-hour round-trip visit to France just to give the official
opening of the exhibition the prestige of his ministerial presence.
And again, Biggs came through.

The Canadian embassy in Paris had hired an automobile for us
and had provided both a trade commissioner to accompany us on
our midmorning drive into northern France and a simultaneous

translator for Hays at the opening ceremony. To accommodate our schedule, the ceremony had been set for about midafternoon. At the appointed time, a small but interested crowd, including the mayor and a member of the Assembly for the district, gathered in the town square outside the unique three-sided barnlike tents Biggs had devised to house the Canadian Holsteins. They listened politely as Hays said, through the interpreter, that he hoped this exhibition herd would mark "the beginning of a new two-way trade between France and Canada."

The ceremony was brief and ended shortly before the regular late-afternoon milking of the cows. Biggs had no use for the milk, so he had let it be known around the community that anyone could get some at the twice-daily milkings. All they had to do was bring their own containers.

At his urging we postponed our return to Paris until the local citizenry began arriving from all directions for the milk. They were mostly housewives and children, and they carried bottles and buckets and kitchen pots and pans of all sizes and shapes. The atmosphere was a little circuslike. The warm camaraderie between Biggs and his two or three helpers and the citizens of Amiens while the Canadians poured the milk into the French containers was moving to witness. Although neither side could fluently communicate with words, there was an obvious communication going on through a mutual instinct for friendship and communion.

The Canadian exhibition, travelling in two semi-trailer trucks with huge Canadian flags—Pearson's new red maple leaf design—painted on their sides, spent the next two months on the road. By November, when they were sold, the Holsteins had been on display at Leuilly-sous-Laon, Le Mans, Tours, Alençon, Metz, Charmoy and Grenoble. Their stops had included several major agricultural shows and a number of artificial insemination units throughout rural France.

At every stop the performance record of each animal was posted on its stall. As Biggs reported to Hays in lengthy letters meticulously handwritten in pencil, some of the French farmers could not believe what they read on the stall postings. So they would come for the actual milkings to witness it for themselves. Once convinced that the performance figures were correct, the farmers began demanding the opportunity to import Canadian Holsteins. The two-way trade Hays forecast that day in Amiens has continued ever since.

Nearly two decades later, the Calgary *Herald*'s Schmidt wrote of the Hays Charolais caper: "History will show this move has kept Canada in the forefront of the world cattle breeding scene." In the years that followed, at least twenty-eight European breeds found their way into Canada through the Hays arrangement. And in September 1980 Hays announced that he was reversing the flow of beef breeding stock that he had introduced with the first importations of Charolais cattle. He had negotiated the sale of fifteen Hays Converter—bred heifers and a bull to a French breeder, Mrs. Schlumberger Primot of Chateau de Grandchamps. (However, French animal health regulations became such an obstacle to getting the animals into France that the deal was not completed.)

In 1982 Syd Williams was unsure which of Hays's developments, the Dairy Commission or his Charolais deal, had the greater impact on Canadian agriculture. He thought the Dairy Commission might have affected more farmers. Yet about the Charolais deal, of one thing he was certain: "It changed the beef industry profoundly, there's no doubt about it whatsoever."

But not to any great personal advantages to Harry Hays, the rancher and breeder. He once wistfully observed, "Had the Hays Converters been on the scene before the Charolais importations, I think they would have taken over the Canadian cattle industry." Yet by then, thanks to his own political initiative, the exotic imports had already stolen much of the thunder from the Hays Converter's genetic impact.

The travelling exhibition herd had proved so successful in opening the French market that another one was planned for Yugoslavia the following year, 1966. Having witnessed the French success, trade and commerce department bureaucrats fought the agriculture department and regained the right to handle the Yugoslav tour, though agriculture still assembled and organized the herd. Among those who stopped to study the stall records of the Canadian animals on display at the annual Novi Sad farm fair that year was the Yugoslav president, Marshal Tito. Canadian Holsteins have been in demand in Yugoslavia, too, ever since.

CHAPTER FOURTEEN

SURPRISE
FACTORS
IN DEFEAT

Harry Hays had been back in Canada from France only a few days when Lester Pearson called the 8 November 1965 election. The Liberal campaign organization was counting heavily on Hays to appeal to the farm voters right across the country, and particularly in western Canada. During the preceding few months, he had become one of the ministers most in demand for speaking engagements to Liberal gatherings, especially in rural ridings. His performance would be crucial to Liberal fortunes on the prairies, where even the Liberal premier of Saskatchewan, Ross Thatcher, was proving more of an obstacle than a help to Liberal success.

Thatcher had annoyed Hays during the spring by giving a speech in Calgary in which he criticized a number of the Pearson government's policies—including a few of Hays's—and made a prediction about the next election. Hays wrote Thatcher a response which did nothing to warm relations between the pair.

"Dear Ross," it began,

> I was interested to learn, from news reports carried the length and breadth of Canada, that you recently went into my home constituency and predicted no seats for the Liberals in Alberta or Saskatchewan in the next federal election.
>
> In a sense I find it encouraging to hear a man of your long political experience making such public comments. Up to now, I had almost begun to believe suggestions that I am Canada's leading novice in politics.
>
> If I must have a foot in my mouth, I would prefer that it be my own.
>
> I assume that you would have no objection now if, the next time I am in Moose Jaw, I comment in similar vein about the future prospects of your government and some of its policies.

In early September Hays launched what was supposed to be his election campaign speaking program at a Lethbridge Liberal nomination convention. Among other issues, he dealt with one he had tackled before—the very current and controversial issue of national unity.

One of the first times Hays had dealt with the issue had been in a speech to a huge annual outdoor gathering at Elk Island Park, near Edmonton, to celebrate Ukrainian Day. It was initially scheduled for a Sunday in late August 1964, but it was rained out—fortunately for Hays. The main purpose of the event, I had discovered quite by accident, was to celebrate the one hundred and fiftieth birthday of a famous Ukrainian poet born into serfdom, Taras Shevchenko. The speech I had prepared for Hays contained no reference to him. We returned for the rescheduled event in September with a substantially rewritten speech.

I knew from my own observations while growing up in Alberta that persons with last names like my mother's—Gerlitz—were known as "bohunks" or "hunkies." They had long been viewed as second-class citizens in western Canada. The Pearson government's drive for national acceptance of linguistic duality and cultural

plurality might gradually bring to Canada a new dimension of tolerance and understanding. Hays was aware of this, and for both of
us, the idea of a country's Parliament deliberately fostering a policy
of diversity, instead of conventional conformity to a single language
and culture, comprised a national purpose of great nobility.

This was the point Hays decided to make in his Ukrainian Day
speech, even though he was well aware how much opposition to
the Pearson bilingualism policy existed among ethnic groups like
the one listening on the grass that day. They considered the
French just another minority ethnic group like themselves, and
they resented the French language being treated as the equal of
English across the country.

"The poetry of Shevchenko lives on," Hays began, "because it
carries in it the truth of human liberty, the truth that all men are
created equal. . . . The most revolutionary idea in our world today
is the idea of equality. . . . This is why we still honour Shevchenko
. . . because he was a poet of freedom."

Hays linked the Pearson government's "unity in diversity" approach to the challenge of Canada's racial and linguistic issues with
Shevchenko's ideals about freedom.

> Canadians need a new understanding of how big was the experiment
> in human co-operation and understanding, in tolerance and self-
> restraint, and in freedom, that the Fathers of Confederation under-
> took when they launched Canada in 1867.
>
> Never before had such differences of race, religion and language
> been settled through responsible discussion at the conference table
> instead of in bloody and destructive civil war. . . . There was some-
> thing even more unusual about Confederation: the fact that two
> races—any two races—should have decided deliberately and peace-
> fully to live side by side without either trying to melt the other down
> into a single cultural pot. This, to me, is what is unique and dis-
> tinctive and valuable about Canada.

Hays believed that the Pearson government's national unity
policy had to be presented, especially in western Canada, as offering personal benefits to all Canadians, regardless of linguistic background. With this in mind, he appealed to his Ukrainian-Canadian
audience's own self-interest. He told them that what they needed

to remember about Canada was that a decision had been reached to let diverse races, religions, languages and cultures grow side by side in freedom and harmony. Canadian freedom, Hays said, was never meant as the freedom to conform to the majority; the lessons of tolerance and understanding, of common sense and self-restraint, were not discriminating. Once learned, they applied to all Canadians, whatever their racial backgrounds, and made life richer and better for all. The Canadian struggle for diversity in freedom was not simply a struggle for survival by French-speaking Canadians or Ukrainian-speaking Canadians. "On the broader stage of the world," said Hays, "it is part of the struggle for survival of all mankind."

Hays's appeal to the self-interest of his twelve-thousand-strong audience was a disappointment. They listened with stolid, unreadable expressions and not a single handclap of applause throughout the speech. They applauded politely but briefly at the end.

The clean-up speaker was the somewhat scandal-smudged mayor of Edmonton, William Hawrelak, a Ukrainian-Canadian himself and a speaker with great natural platform charisma. Using English and Ukrainian, but no French, he brought the vast crowd instantly to applauding life. Hays departed, certain he had not made a single convert.

He had little reason to expect that the audience of Lethbridge Liberals would receive the national unity message any more enthusiastically than the Elk Island Ukrainians had. He was painfully aware—even while understanding the practical political motivation behind it—of how skillfully western Tories were playing their two-faced language policy game. While piously supporting, for the benefit of Quebec voters, recognition of English and French as Canada's official languages in Parliament, western Tory M.P.s lost no opportunity in private gatherings in their home constituencies to criticize the Liberals for "forcing French down our throats," as it was so often and so demagogically put.

Although most of the Tories knew as well as Liberals how important the issue was to keeping Quebec in Canada, the temptation to capitalize on the racial and religious prejudices still prevalent across the west and play them off against the Liberals was more than any average politician could resist. Hays knew that many nominal western supporters of the Liberal party felt much the same way. They could hardly help it, since day after day, month after month, they heard little but negative, misleading and often highly emotive opposition to the policy, including plenty from provincial-level politicians as well.

In his speech to the Lethbridge Liberals, Hays struck at this aspect of the Pearson government's political problem in western Canada, where the most skillful player of the Tories' two-faced official languages position was John Diefenbaker.

Hays stated that the central issue of the election was nothing less than Canada itself. The most important decision Canadians would make in this election was whether to "save their country through the exercise of reason and moderation and that maturity that marks the truly civilized nation, or whether they [were] going to let emotions and the black prejudices of the jungle take over and blow their country apart."

Although he cautiously side-stepped any mention of his name, Hays shifted his attack towards Diefenbaker with an oblique reference to widespread opposition, from a number of leading Conservatives who publicly supported the Pearson policy, to Diefenbaker's "one Canada" posture, which implied his opposition to official bilingualism even while he claimed to support it. "It is not Mr. Pearson who is willing to set province against province, race against race, for the sake of cheap partisan political gains or the hope of such gains. . . . Don't take my word for it. Ask some of the responsible leaders of Conservatism in this country where the biggest contribution to unity has come from."

Hays was visibly unwell that night, though it probably would not have made any difference to the unenthusiastic reception his speech received. As soon as we could, we excused ourselves and got him to bed at a local motel (one we now had enough political experience to ensure was owned by a prominent financial supporter of the Liberals).

We had arranged for a single-engined plane to fly us next morning from Lethbridge to Banff, where Hays was scheduled at noon to give a major speech to the annual meeting of the Canadian Agricultural Chemicals Association. Hays did not mention his illness that morning while we waited to board the plane, but he was unusually silent. He took the rear seat, and as we flew northward, he tried to sleep. As we approached Calgary, Hays tapped me on the shoulder. He told me that he was feeling too unwell to go on with this journey. He wanted the pilot to land and let him off in Calgary. Then I should fly on to Banff and deliver the speech on his behalf from the text we had already prepared. It was Friday, and he could spend the weekend recovering.

This I proceeded to do. Neither of us had any inkling at the time that this was the beginning of the end of Harry Hays's career as a federal cabinet minister.

Hays did not have a doctor examine him. He went home and spent the weekend in bed. Back in Ottawa on Monday, he said he felt much better, and he plunged into his heavy schedule with as much energy as ever. On 23 September he was nominated again as the Liberal candidate in his Calgary South riding. He discovered that morning that his riding organizers had not done as much work at getting a good turnout as he had expected. He spent several hours on the telephone himself ensuring that there would be a respectable crowd at a meeting that evening.

His campaign schedule steadily became more demanding. On Tuesday, 12 October, he spoke to an evening meeting in Dauphin, Manitoba. Then we drove back to Winnipeg for the night, flew to Toronto the next morning and drove to Millikin in North York, where Hays participated in the official opening of an international plowing match at the Massey-Ferguson farm. We drove back to Toronto airport that evening and flew to Edmonton. We were scheduled to fly by private plane the next morning to meetings in Dawson Creek and Fort St. John in northern British Columbia, fly back to Edmonton that night and spend Friday travelling by helicopter to meetings in Mayerthorpe and Stoney Plain in northern Alberta.

Hays did not say very much on the long flight from Toronto to Edmonton Wednesday night, nor on the long taxi ride in to the city from the airport. As usual I checked us into the hotel and collected two keys to his suite, one for him and the other to give me access to the sitting room. We went up to his suite and briefly discussed the next day's schedule, and I gave him speech material for the meetings. He said he would have a meal sent up to his room and talk on the telephone to some of his family who were visiting his sister Virginia, who lived in Edmonton, and then get to bed early.

Early the next morning there was no answer when I knocked on his door. I used my key to the sitting room and found the suite empty. A note on the coffee table asked me to call Virginia. She told me that she and other relatives had come to visit Hays the night before and had been so concerned by how ill he appeared that they had insisted he visit the emergency ward at an Edmonton hospital. A doctor had quickly diagnosed a severe case of pneumonia. Hays had evidently been suffering from it at least since the Lethbridge speech more than a month earlier.

There was nothing to be done about that day's meetings in northern British Columbia except cancel them. Edmonton Senator J. Harper Prowse, a former Alberta Liberal party leader, substituted for Hays at the meetings scheduled the following day in Mayerthorpe and Stoney Plain. The turnouts in those rural communities did not bode well for election success. The Mayerthorpe lunch meeting had mistakenly been advertised as an evening meeting, and the Stoney Plain evening meeting had been announced as the lunch meeting, and nobody noticed the mistake until that morning. There was an audience of nine at Mayerthorpe and two at Stoney Plain.

In Ottawa, Finance Minister Walter Gordon, the national campaign chairman, said at a news conference the day after Hays went to hospital that the Liberal party had suffered the "biggest blow" of the election campaign when it had learned that the agriculture minister was ill. "He was our best campaigner in rural areas. Naturally, we're disappointed."

There was some hope that Hays would recover quickly and soon return to the national campaign trail. He himself hoped to be able to get home to Calgary sometime during that weekend and at least resume some campaigning in his own riding the following week.

But the cards of fortune held a different fate for him. The drugs the doctors had given him to bring the pneumonia under control had virtually eliminated his immunity to any other diseases, rendering him susceptible to the most virulent forms of virtually any affliction anyone in the same room might have. He had to remain in strict isolation.

As it turned out, he was not allowed to leave the Edmonton hospital for nearly two weeks. And even when he could finally be flown to Calgary in a government aircraft, he had to be taken to the plane and to his home by ambulance and had to remain isolated in his bedroom. All of his scheduled appearances across the country in support of the Pearson government's farm policies had to be cancelled. Nor was he able to make any campaign appearances even in his own riding, except for a brief appearance at a news conference in his living room about three days before election day.

◻   ◻   ◻

The Pearson government's national medicare plan was the major recognized campaign issue in Hays's riding of Calgary South, though the anti-French racial issue was also actively working against him beneath the surface. There was sharp irony for Hays in the anti-medicare campaign that he had to contend with from his sickbed. Its leader and most vociferous opponent had once been Hays's political hero.

Alberta's Social Credit premier Ernest C. Manning's attack against medicare included a lengthy television statement that he paid to have carried on stations across the country. It was also printed in booklet form and widely distributed as "An objective analysis of the proposed Federal Medicare Scheme."

Manning favoured what he called "a superior alternative to the federal proposal"—a mixture of private and government subsidized insurance schemes in which some sort of means test—he was obscure on this point—would determine who could afford to pay their own medical protection costs and who could not. He particularly objected to the provision in Pearson's proposal requiring universal coverage. This meant that, by compulsion if necessary, every citizen must be covered with the plan's protection in provinces accepting the federal contribution of 50 per cent of the cost. Manning warned that if Canadians permitted implementation of the Pearson medicare plan, the inevitable result would be "a nation turned into a regimented socialistic welfare state" from which there would be no turning back.

Manning, arrogant with Alberta's expanding petroleum wealth and his born-again Christian's all-consuming faith in his own inner voice, decided finally that Alberta taxpayers should forgo the millions in federal contributions for a universal public medicare scheme in his province, and he imposed his own self-styled "superior" plan, a voluntary, prepaid, state-subsidized medical insurance program. It was such a disastrous confusion, with payments to doctors sometimes behind by as much as fourteen months, that it helped defeat his successor, Social Crediter Harry Strom, and convinced Albertans that they wanted to join all other Canadians in the Pearson medicare plan.

In the 1965 election campaign in Calgary South, Manning's cry of socialist medicine had to be taken seriously. Hays's prospects were not helped by the fact that leaders of the Alberta Medical Society also went on radio twice during the campaign with two-hour hotline radio forums attacking the Pearson medicare plan. Hays was able to tape a handful of radio commercials in support of his campaign, and one of them tried, in fifty-two seconds, to offet Manning's anti-medicare attack.

"This is Harry Hays," the commercial, read by Hays, began.

Premier Manning says your federal government's medicare proposals would rob Albertans of their personal freedom. I've always respected Premier Manning. But on this issue I think he's wrong. Sickness can put anyone except the very rich right into the poorhouse without a minute's warning. There isn't much personal freedom in the poorhouse. That's why Mr. Pearson's government is offering to pay half the cost of your doctor bills, if your provincial government will pay the other half.

Your federal government believes you should be able to go to a doctor when you need to, whether you can afford it or not. But our constitution makes medicare the responsibility of your provincial government. And Premier Manning doesn't want your provincial government to pay half your doctor bills. He thinks you should be free to look after them yourself. But nine other provinces want our plan, not Mr. Manning's, and Mr. Manning will probably change his mind if you vote for our government.

Columnist Charles Lynch interviewed Hays as election day approached. Hays told him that the part of his federal political career he had enjoyed most was administering the agriculture department: "I've learned a great deal in the last couple of years, and there sure was a lot for me to learn." He predicted that there would be some surprises in rural Canada on election day. "I think our farm program is getting through to the farmer, and everywhere we have a good candidate, we could win."

Sickness did not dampen his sense of humour. He admitted that not all Liberal candidates were top-drawer. This was because it was difficult to get the best man in a constituency to run. "Usually their wives talk them out of it," he said, eyeing Muriel with a grin. "We had a pretty good way of life going before we got messed up in all this business. I'm not sure she really wants me to get re-elected." Muriel assured him that she did, but more than that she wanted him alive and well.

"You'd get another," he teased her.

"I don't want another. I want you."

Lynch described the campaign being carried on under the guiding eyes of campaign manager Ed O'Connor as "folksy" and mentioned a Hays ad that claimed he had "carried Calgary's name to the highest councils of our nation in true western style." Lynch closed his column by saying that Hays's "enforced withdrawal from the last month of the campaign [had] been a sore blow to Liberal hopes in the west."

And Lynch was right. Without Hays to sell the government's farm program to the rural electorate, the outlook was dim. There were few others in the Pearson cabinet with enough appreciation of what Hays had been trying to do for farmers to make any real impact, including the prime minister himself.

Several days before Pearson was due to begin campaigning in Saskatchewan, at Hays's suggestion I telephoned Tom Kent, a leading strategist and influence in the Prime Minister's Office. I told him that both Hays and I believed the prime minister should concentrate on agricultural as well as national unity issues in western Canada. Kent agreed and suggested that I write some material on the agricultural policies Hays had been putting forward and bring them to Edmonton for Pearson.

I worked hard for two or three days on the material. I sent it to Hays in his isolation, and he gave his approval. I flew to Edmonton and waited in an outer room of Pearson's Macdonald Hotel suite until he returned from his evening meeting. It was nearly midnight before I was ushered in to see him. He asked with genuine concern after Hays and said what a tragedy for the government it was that he had become sick and was unable to campaign. I conveyed to him Hays's own regrets and good wishes and then informed him that I had prepared some material for him, at Hays's suggestion, on farm issues for use during his western swing.

Perhaps it was the late hour, but Pearson frowned at my words and half threw up his hands. He said that he had promised to speak out on the national unity issues in the same terms during this campaign no matter what part of the country he was in, and he intended to keep that promise.

I tried to suggest that he could do that and still talk about the agricultural issues important to western Canadians, but he cut me off with polite impatience by saying that he could not on such short notice incorporate new material, especially on issues with which he was unfamiliar. Even Kent was unable to change the prime minister's mind. Pearson campaigned across the prairies on the national unity issues, just as he had promised in Quebec that he would, and ignored agriculture almost completely.

It is doubtful that anything Pearson might have said on farm policies would have made any difference to the election outcome in Calgary South. What almost certainly would have made all the difference necessary for Harry Hays's electoral survival would have been his own presence in the campaign. But that was not possible, and on election night, the difference Hays's illness made was his defeat. The margin was maddeningly slender. Social Credit tactics may have been just enough to have ensured that margin.

The election night ballot count showed Hays losing by 159 votes to Tory Ray Ballard. A total of 466 ballots were spoiled, many because voters had marked an X beside both Hays's name and that of the Social Credit candidate, an L. Pearson. (At that time, the name of a candidate's party was not printed on the ballot; only the candidate's name appeared.) The vote was close enough that Hays called for a judicial recount. But the results of that were only more maddeningly close: the margin of his defeat, including the armed forces votes, was reduced to seventy-eight votes.

The same day that result was published, Hays had a private lunch with Pearson at 24 Sussex Drive to discuss his future. They talked at length in a most enjoyable way about a wide variety of subjects, including the possibility of Hays remaining on as minister of agriculture in the Senate and other hypothetical futures for him. But never once did the prime minister allow the conversation to stray even close to a concrete decision on what he wanted to happen to Hays. Apparently Pearson had not yet made up his mind on that question. Hays was deeply impressed by Pearson's easy skill at manipulating the parameters of a conversation. While still, for the time being at least, minister of agriculture, Hays flew back to

Calgary that afternoon with his future still very much in doubt.

Hays by then had many farm policy programs in various stages of development, and he would have enjoyed the opportunity to complete the establishment of the national Dairy Commission he had worked so hard to design. Pearson's government had failed to win the majority it had sought; except for one seat, it was unrepresented in Saskatchewan and Alberta. Given Hays's qualifications, I believed it would have been sensible for the prime minister to appoint Hays to the Senate while allowing him to remain agriculture minister long enough to implement the main items of legislation he had ready, including the establishment of the Dairy Commission.

Hays had, in fact, received a telephone call the day after his election defeat from William Stewart, Ontario's minister of agriculture, urging him to find some way of remaining on until he could get the Dairy Commission legislation through Parliament. Both the Ontario and Quebec ministries of agriculture had come to share Hays's belief that this was the only long-term hope for a healthy dairy industry across Canada. Concern was indicated to Hays immediately after his defeat that without him in the federal ministry, the Dairy Commission plan might go awry.

Hays enjoyed recounting another phone call he received the day after his defeat. Some long-time farmer friends from his home-town area of Carstairs called to tell him how sorry and disappointed they were that he would no longer be in the Commons as agriculture minister, because they thought he had been doing such a hell of a good job. Hays thanked them and then asked who they had voted for. Why, they informed him, they had of course voted for Tory Eldon Woolliams, the Calgary lawyer representing their Bow River riding, because he was always telling them how much he helped his good friend Harry get things through Parliament down there in Ottawa.

I took the information about Hays's representations from Ontario and Quebec agricultural authorities and my Senate proposition to Jim Coutts, prime ministerial appointments secretary, and tried to persuade him to pursue it with Pearson. To my surprise, Coutts vigorously disagreed with my view that it was a politically practical move. He argued that the voters had exercised their judgement on Hays's farm policies by rejecting them, and their decision must be accepted.

I told Coutts that his argument was just short of preposterous, especially when it was considered that Hays's illness had prevented him from campaigning in support of his policies and that not even the prime minister had been prepared to try to make up for this. Coutts stood firm.

"It's too bad, but Harry Hays and his agriculture policies have been rejected. It would be arrogant to ignore this and appoint him to the Senate as minister of agriculture. Harry's a wonderful guy. It was a good idea, and we made a good try. But it didn't work out, and now we've got to start all over again."

Bitterly disappointed, I gave up the argument, certain that Coutts's view would prevail with the prime minister. A chance meeting with Tom Kent lifted my spirits a little. He was strongly in favour of keeping Hays on. He thought the best approach might be to make Hays a Senate minister without portfolio assigned to work with a new minister of agriculture in the Commons.

When I mentioned this to Hays, however, he did not think it would work. Evidently the idea had been touched upon in his wide-ranging luncheon conversation with Pearson, and Hays had told the prime minister the same thing. Pearson had told him that if they tried anything from the Senate, he would prefer to keep Hays on there as minister of agriculture. But he had carefully avoided indicating what he might finally do about Hays's defeat. There was nothing to be done except wait for the prime minister to decide.

CHAPTER FIFTEEN

MANIPULATIONS AND FAREWELLS

Harry Hays resigned from his cabinet post in December 1965, went on a Hawaiian holiday to recuperate from his pneumonia, and was appointed to the Senate by Prime Minister Pearson on 24 February 1966. Although he never served in cabinet again, he retained his influence on Liberal governments' farm policies and remained a respected, if resented, Liberal party power broker in Alberta for the rest of his days.

After his election defeat, Hays wasted little time on regret and disappointment, though undoubtedly it was the biggest single disappointment of his life. Had he won, he would have been a very powerful person. So he had lost a great deal when he lost the election by a mere seventy-eight votes. He loved the challenge that being minister of agriculture presented and felt that he was just beginning to hit his stride in the position. But that challenge was gone now, and Hays would have to look for new ones.

One of the most generous tributes to Hays on his defeat came in a November Calgary *Herald* editorial which said that Hays's many capabilities would be missed in the political worlds of Calgary and Canada. His political career had been "distinguished by the energy and selflessness devoted to it [and had been] characterized by the finest traditions of public service. . . . It is unfortunate that the ends of politics are not always productive."

Calgary journalist-historian James H. Gray wrote in the Ottawa *Citizen* that there was little doubt that the all-out war of organized medicine on the medicare scheme had been largely responsible for Hays's defeat. Gray said that although Premier Manning had had a role in this, he had got his come-uppance.

> On one point, everybody can stop worrying. The threat of Premier E. C. Manning to become a new force in federal politics has gone forever, taken care of by Premier Manning himself. . . . Not only did Manning fail to exercise his magic on the electors, the Social Credit candidates in several ridings did worse with his help in this election than they had done without it in 1963.

The most extensive analysis of Hays's defeat was written by the Calgary *Albertan*'s Ottawa correspondent, the brilliant Alberta-born Joyce Fairbairn, later Prime Minister Trudeau's long-time legislative assistant and a senator. She reported that Hays "wrapped his electoral disappointment in the cloth of matter-of-fact philosophy which is his trademark."

"I've got no excuses," he told her. "Elections are elections, and you've got to let the chips fall where they may. The people have spoken, and that's our democracy, isn't it?" He had difficulty understanding the Liberal shutout on the prairies of all but one seat. "We brought in good programs and had good policies. But maybe the people don't understand policies. Maybe programs don't mean much when it comes to voting."

Fairbairn reported that more deadly than nonexposure because of Hays's illness was the relentless campaign waged by Manning against the Liberal medicare scheme—"He made a pretty strong plea," Hays said, "and that hurt me quite a bit."

"Apart from constituting a political wound to the Liberals," Fairbairn wrote,

Hays will also leave a void in Parliament. He was not wholly appreciated by all his 264 colleagues. On the other hand he could never be accused of inducing boredom or lethargy in anyone who crossed his orbit. . . . There were no airs, no façades. He was and remains practical, down-to-earth and earthy. He expounded crisply on everything from complicated policy and national unity to cows' udders and artificial insemination. Sometimes his graphic explanations were beyond the pale of a family newspaper.

There are many dedicated men in Parliament. There are few stimulating characters. Hays was one of those few, and his sharp wit and gruff charm will be missed.

The election result wiped out forever Hays's naiveté about the important role in politics of legitimate government patronage. Defeated party candidates and other Liberals across the prairies had been rightly disappointed, frustrated and annoyed by Hays's refusal while minister to play the conventional patronage game. There were various jobs and contracts, especially legal work, that were not only his right but his responsibility to assign to someone. Everything else being equal, Liberals could do the work as well as Tories, and it is politically wise to give such recognition to supporters rather than opponents whenever decently possible. By refusing to switch the Tory assignees he found in place when he took over the ministry, Hays left this patronage in the hands of Liberal detractors, thereby not gaining their support and probably losing some support from disappointed and angered Liberals.

However, Hays gradually came to change his mind about patronage. He had discovered from the election campaign that, like power, patronage could not be ignored. Either it was used for one's own purposes or one's opponents used it for theirs. Patronage could not be neutralized—nor even entirely eliminated. He grew disillusioned about the failure of his no-patronage approach. He knew that he had alienated a lot of Liberals by not giving patronage jobs or contracts to them. But he had also learned that many of the people he had kept on in their Tory patronage jobs and contracts, though displaying discreet nonpartisanship between elections, had openly worked against him and other Liberals once the election was called.

Once in the Senate and a Liberal party bagman in charge of patronage in Alberta, Hays never forgot this lesson. He said that if he were given the chance, he would handle patronage very differently now. He would, for example, say to a lawyer, "All right, here's so much patronage, and we want this much work from you, and if you don't come through, it goes to somebody else. The people willing to do the work are the people who get it, and anybody who doesn't come through just gets struck off the list." Senator Harry Hays handled Liberal government patronage in Alberta in this manner for the rest of his days, regardless of whether people approved or not.

Hays quickly learned how to conduct himself with the dignity befitting a senator. With informal advice, he helped his immediate successor, Minister of Agriculture J. J. ("Joe") Greene, to establish the Dairy Commission. He continued to maintain some influence on government agricultural policies as a member of the Liberal parliamentary caucus and on the national agricultural scene through activities of the Senate Agriculture Committee, especially after he succeeded Senator Hazen Argue as its chairman in 1980.

He also had more time to spend on his ranch than he had while a cabinet minister. There he tended to his farm business, went riding or drove in his pony buggy. "I only go walking," he joked, "if I can walk slow and take lots of stops." If Hays held one tenet of faith about human existence above any other, it was a belief in the power and satisfaction of material wealth. One of his favourite sayings was his own rustic version of the proverb, "He who pays the piper calls the tune"; Hays's version was: "The keeper of the kapoo calls the tune."

From his wide reading, Hays had accumulated countless odds and ends of interesting knowledge. Drawing from this storehouse, he was once able to deal with a coyote problem on his ranch. Coyotes study the movements of all living things, especially human beings, within their territory. Those around his ranch therefore knew that Hays rose at five in the morning and that if they wanted to raid his sheep flock with immunity, they would be wise to do it at three or four o'clock. When Hays began to notice a sheep or a lamb occasionally missing from his flock, he knew that if coyotes were the culprits, he would have to get up even earlier to catch them.

And so, at three in the morning, he crept into a concealed place overlooking the sheep pasture. He did not have to wait long before three coyotes, with tongues lolling, came trotting into the flock. Hays watched with fascination as the sheep welcomed the intruders like their own kind, even letting the coyotes rub against them. While two of the coyotes kept up their pretended flirtation, Hays noticed the third coyote edging towards a young lamb standing a little way off from the main flock. Behaving in a playful manner, the coyote skillfully nudged the lamb farther away and down a slope, until both were out of sight of the other sheep. Then with vicious swiftness the coyote was at the lamb's throat, killing it without a sound. Within moments the two other coyotes joined the killer, and they silently made off with their prize, the surviving sheep none the wiser.

Hays returned to the same spot at the same time the next morning with a rifle and with a few badly aimed shots drove off the surprised coyotes. They never returned.

Once settled in the Senate, Hays kept himself busy. One year he was offered a position on Canada's team of parliamentary representatives to the United Nations. He accepted and spent several weeks in New York attending sessions of various U.N. bodies. Muriel Hays remembered how much he came to enjoy New York City, its infinite variety of human activity and endless energy. "He told me he could be quite happy living there, once he got used to it," she said.

Early in his marriage to Margaret Sinclair, Pierre Trudeau, she and their first son, Justin, spent a long weekend as guests on the Hays ranch. It was winter, and Hays took Trudeau horseback riding across the snow-covered ranch lands. "It is a joy to remember it and the enthusiasm and earthiness of the guy," Trudeau recalled.

Harry insisted that I visit a Hutterite colony in the neighbourhood. It was quite an eye-opener for me, and I think he did it for that reason, because he thought it was an important broadening of my political understanding of western Canada. Or maybe it was a subconscious desire on his part to share his view of Canada with me. Harry never preached a lot of grand ideas, but he acted them out. He lived them. He was a great guy.

Muriel gave Trudeau a tour of the ranch quarters. "I remember she had this enormous freezer filled with an incredible number of goodies." One of Hays's hobbies was cooking. He also collected recipes, some of them copied in his own handwriting or pasted into a tattered school scribbler. On the first page of the scribbler are two recipes for dandelion wine. On other early pages are recipes for Dad's Cookies, Goose Stuffing, Lemon Pudding, Divinity Fudge, Clifford Tea Cakes, Carmel Toffee, Chinese Chews and Million Dollar Cake. There are also notes on how best to cook a leg of lamb, a turkey, a duck, a prime rib of beef and a pigeon. Under a 9 May 1971 date is the menu served to eighteen people, including a visiting delegation of Yugoslavs. At the end Hays wrote: "Served Medoc Cruise—red wine (French)."

The last entry is dated 25 December 1980, Hays's birthday. It briefly describes how the turkey for that Christmas Day's dinner was cooked and concludes: "I am 71 years old. I find every turkey different, including the turkeys in the press."

◻   ◻   ◻

Even after years of moderating experience in Parliament and the Senate, Hays's lifelong penchant for mischief could still get him into political hot water, as it did in November 1980. Hays had been selected co-chairman (with Quebecker Serge Joyal) of the Special Joint Parliamentary Committee on the Constitution, a role that would prove to be one of his last and most exhausting in public life. That fall the committee was engaged in holding nationwide public hearings on the constitutional reforms included in Prime Minister Trudeau's patriation package.

The committee had just heard a joint presentation from the National Action Committee on the Status of Women and the Canadian Advisory Committee on the Status of Women. The formal committee hearing had actually ended for the day. Among the women preparing to leave was Doris Anderson, a leading voice in the cause of Canadian women. She also happened to be a relative of Muriel Hays and a former federal Liberal candidate.

Meaning it only as light, informal, off-the-record banter, Hays said to Anderson: "I'm just wondering why we don't have a section in here [the Constitution] about babies and children. All you girls will be out working, and we're not going to have anybody to look after them."

According to Hays, Anderson "was not the least bit annoyed. However, her colleagues were." His words were picked up by the news media and reported as though he had been serious. They produced an overnight sensation across the land. Delegates at a Red Deer conference of the Alberta Status of Women Action Committee voted unanimously to censure Hays. They termed his remarks "insulting," "ignorant" and "extremely sexist." Premier Richard Hatfield of New Brunswick said that Hays's words were "just an indication to the women of Canada of how much work they have to do." The premier hoped that they also represented "a view that has since gone by the boards."

Columnist Allan Fotheringham reported that Hays became "a cult figure in less than a week. The letters-to-the-editor columns are aflame with his name, and editorial writers furrow their brows in angst at his mere mention." Probably the most hostile attack came from Toronto *Sun* columnist Laura Sabia, a defeated federal Conservative candidate. She called Hays "a witless wonder from the Senate" and a "Methuselahan buffoon from the patronage pork barrel of the Liberals." She summed up his words as "the rambling waggeries of fossilized thinkers."

In private, Hays was mostly amused by the furore. He received as many letters supporting his words as criticizing them; his Senate mail ran two-to-one in support.

Hays never apologized for his remark. "I won't take anything back," he said. "My comment showed that I'm concerned about who will look after the children of Canada, and I'm still concerned. It's something that society has to try and work out quickly."

One of the less publicized reforms in Trudeau's package, and one that did not draw Hays into any trouble, was the fundamental dilution of the Senate's power of absolute veto over any legislation put forward by the House of Commons—a power the Senate had enjoyed since Confederation. This reform limited to 180 days the length of time that the Senate could hold up any constitutional change it might oppose, even changes to the nature of the Senate itself. Hays played an unsung but vital role as a tactical consultant to Minister of Justice Jean Chrétien in persuading his fellow senators to agree to this reduction in their parliamentary might.

Hays knew all his fellow senators well, and Chrétien found his evaluations very helpful. The pair used to go down a list of senators, trying to judge how each would vote on relinquishing Senate veto power. Chrétien recalled: "Harry would say of this one, 'If Prime Minister Trudeau asked him to jump off a bridge, he would do it without hesitating. When he was ten feet from hitting the water, he might ask himself why the prime minister wanted him to do it. But he would jump.' " Of another senator, Hays said that he, too, would jump off a bridge if the prime minister asked him to, but he would be too loyal even to wonder why.

Among Hays's more impassioned, though private, critics during this period were his sister Laura, who refused to speak to him for several years because of his support for Trudeau and his Constitution, and his sister Catherine, who wrote to him saying that she could hardly hold her head up among mutual friends in Calgary, so ashamed was she of his politics.

Catherine first congratulated him on his remarks about the "girls." "I along with everyone I know both young and old, male and female agree. And they all admire your guts for coming out and saying so." Then she lowered her political boom on him.

She told Hays that everyone had hoped he was at last going to stand up and be counted, but so far, she feared, they thought he was selling them out in the west. "They had all thought that you would be the only voice for the west, and they all know you could get our point across if you weren't a pawn of Trudeau's." She said that while only the women in the east were mad at him, in the west everybody was mad. "You used to be Senator Harry Hays, now it's Good ol' Harry, Stupid ol' Harry and every other insulting thing they can think of. You used to have the respect as well as the affection of a lot of these people."

Her husband had listened to criticism at the Kiwanis; her son's Rotary Club tore Hays apart. "Every social evening event we attend, people let us know in no uncertain terms what they think." She stressed that she did not want politics to come between them, that he was her brother as well as her friend. But,

> nobody here can understand how you could be your own man in every other undertaking . . . and now with the biggest opportunity of

your life to hold this country together you are going along with those bent on our destruction. If it's too late to save face, I would suggest finding some way of resigning before your good reputation is completely gone. . . .

You know as well as I do you are a self-made man, and if you are bent on destroying what you have built up at least do it yourself, not as a pawn of a clever, selfish man who cares not a damn who he uses to accomplish what he has set out to dô.

In his lengthy and concerned response, Hays said of political life: "Publicly the road is always rough or you are just a rubber stamp." He reminded Catherine of how, when he was mayor, he had insisted on giving Calgary a single local government by annexing all its suburbs. "This was the first unpopular thing I did in public life. Everyone advised me [I] couldn't win even though it was right." He also reminded her that the first time he ran for mayor, their sister Virginia and her husband not only voted for his opponent but provided ten automobiles from the brother-in-law's own used-car dealership to drive others to the polls to vote against Hays.

He hoped that the joint committee could eventually report to both Houses with a package that history would acclaim as a noble and well thought-out document. And he affirmed, with characteristic purpose, "No, I will not resign but will fight on for what I sincerely hope is just and right. . . . Hopefully we will do as good a job as Sir John A. Macdonald and his people did so long ago."

□   □   □

Hays and I kept in touch as friends for the rest of his days, but after his defeat as minister of agriculture, we had only one adventure together in politics. Between us, we helped to invent Rod Sykes as mayor of Calgary, though there were moments afterwards when we would wonder whether we had also created a local political monster.

By August of 1969 candidates were beginning to jockey for position in the campaign for the civic election that October. The man Hays had defeated in Calgary South in 1963, Jack Leslie, was completing his second term as mayor and was generally expected to run for a third term. When some friends raised the possibility of Hays returning to civic politics, he first said that he did not want to be Calgary's mayor again. He laughed: "Muriel and the rest of the family have said they'll leave me if I even consider it." But he shared with many others in the city a frustration over the drifting inaction and indirection that he felt characterized the Leslie regime, and at last he consented to enter the race if no one better than Leslie turned up.

I was then managing editor of the Calgary *Albertan*. Hays and I discussed the idea and decided to float a trial balloon and see where the winds of fortune carried it. The next morning the *Albertan* ran an unbylined story on the front page that said, "A move is afoot to persuade Harry Hays to return to the civic political wars from the serenity of the Senate in this fall's municipal election. . . . While [Hays] did not say yes, neither did he say a flat no to an approach on the idea of returning to the civic arena in the October election."

Hays's telephone rang off the hook for several days afterward, with people urging him to plunge into the campaign and offering their support. Despite his initial reluctance, Hays was preparing to give the idea serious thought. But a chance remark heard at a cocktail party turned out to be a crucial influence.

In September I attended a reception of *Time* magazine's editors. I was among a group chatting about the civic election campaign. With us was Ruth-Margaret Ogle, the outspoken wife of *Time*'s long-serving western Canada editor, Ed Ogle. Ruth-Margaret— whose opinions I trusted—was saying that as annoying and grating as freshman aldermanic candidate Rod Sykes could be at times, he was in her judgement a competent, intelligent and honest man. "If he were running for mayor, he's the one I'd vote for. As much as I can't stand him."

If Sykes had impressed Ruth-Margaret, then he must be impressive. I recounted this news to Hays, who was involving himself deeper and deeper with Calgary's civic politics. He said only that he knew Sykes—head of the CPR's Calgary-based real estate subsidiary, Marathon Realty Ltd.—and agreed that he was very competent.

By then Hays had indicated at a news conference that he was ready and willing to enter the mayoralty race if enough Calgarians wanted him to. He had also taken a few swipes at the sitting mayor. "You can't be a social butterfly and be the mayor," he said. He had also taken a poke at Leslie's Tory political partisanship over city hall issues. "You can't clobber the senior governments one day, then turn around and ask them for favours the next day. There is no room for that in civic government."

Towards the end of September, however, Hays telephoned me late one night to say that he had looked at things realistically and had decided that he could not possibly be mayor of Calgary and a senator at the same time. His family were all dead against it, and so he was going to announce that he could not, after all, entertain the possibility of running. Hays asked me to pass on to Sykes his advice that he drop out of the aldermanic race and enter the race for the mayor's job. "Tell him he'll only find being an alderman frustrating because all you can do as an alderman is talk. Tell him he should go for the whole bundle. And tell him if he does, I'll drop out and announce I'm backing him."

The message was conveyed. By morning, Sykes had decided to take Hays's advice. We arranged that the *Albertan* would publish the exclusive news that Sykes was switching from the aldermanic to the mayoralty race, followed the next morning with the further exclusive news that Hays had dropped from the running and was instead putting his support behind Sykes.

"I have decided to publicly support Rod Sykes," Hays said in a speech a few nights later, "because I think he knows how to get things done, and to get things done for all the people of Calgary, not just a few who enjoy the privilege of having friends at city hall." With this, Sykes's winning campaign against Leslie was launched. Although not universally beloved, Sykes would prove to be a competent mayor. However, his political career would also become one of the most vitriol-splashed in recent Canadian history because of a chronic inability to resist making caustic comments when a kindly one might have sufficed. But Hays had no way of foreseeing that at the time.

□　　□　　□

During his years in the Senate, Hays continued to advocate producer-managed marketing systems for the selling of farm products. His conservative critics saw this as his conversion to left-wing liberal thinking—because of his long association with the Liberal party—when it was really a reflection of his inherent conservatism.

Hays saw producer-controlled marketing systems as the best, probably even the only, means of ensuring the survival of the family farm, that most vital and fundamental form of any free enterprise market system and the primary source of society's most essential resource—food. Just as he had seen Pearson's medicare policy not as socialism but as the only practical way to conserve individual freedom of access to medical treatment, Hays saw farm marketing systems as the only practical way of conserving free enterprise by keeping the family farm profitable enough to be workable.

On 30 April 1982, Hays was scheduled to preside over another meeting of the Senate Agriculture Committee as it considered the final report of an extensive study of beef marketing systems. As Hays later told his farm business partner and former deputy minister, Syd Williams, he awoke in his Ottawa apartment at his usual 5 A.M. and went to the bathroom to take a shower. As he reached down for the soap, a sudden sharp pain struck him in the chest. Nearly two hours later, Williams received a phone call.

> I'd had a sore back, and Hays said, "Syd, how's your back?" That's the kind of a thoughtful man he always was. "Oh, not bad," I said. He said, "Syd, I'm in trouble. I didn't think I'd make it back to the bed. I've been lying here hoping it would go away and it hasn't gone away."

Williams immediately called an ambulance; Hays underwent heart surgery the following Tuesday, 4 May. He died in the recovery room without regaining consciousness. He was seventy-two years old.

"He was always careful about his health," Muriel said later. "The day before, he was as healthy as you or me. Then he had this heart attack and he was gone in five days."

On 10 May, following a funeral service attended by some four hundred mourners, including Jean Chrétien, Senator Bud Olson, Jim Coutts, Joyce Fairbairn and other Ottawa dignitaries, in Calgary's Roman Catholic St. Mary's Cathedral, Hays was buried in the Carstairs cemetery near other members of his family, including his Uncle Dan who had in earlier times spent so many years in the beer parlour of the local hotel.

There were many tributes to Hays. Probably as lasting a tribute as any came from one of his successors in the agriculture portfolio, fellow Albertan and senator Bud Olson. Remembering how often as Trudeau's minister of agriculture he had consulted Hays, Olson described him as a "very, very reliable source of advice—I don't know anybody who was on that plane. Harry was the kind of a person that regarded problems as challenges to be solved, not things that would defeat your purpose."

"He was very shrewd, intuitive," Senator Keith Davey said of him.

He had an intuitive understanding of politics. Politics in the final analysis is people, and Harry was interested in people. He had a fine nose for political realities. You could spend a lot of money on a survey, and he could tell you the answers free. I think while he was in Ottawa he moved from being a populist right-winger to being genuinely a Liberal middle-of-the-roader. The word *Liberal* is anathema in Alberta. Not many people as they grow older become more liberal; here was a guy from Alberta who did.

Walter Gordon remembered of Hays: "He was a very good politician. In fact, I liked everything about him. I liked particularly his forthrightness."

"Harry was a kind of a scientist," remembered Marie Kennedy, wife of his long-time friend and associate Charlie.

He had a very scientific mind. He could have been a doctor, he could have been a lawyer—anything. He had that kind of personality. He had a wonderful gift for people, and people always came to him. People just leaned on him. He would listen. He was a wonderful listener. He had wonderful hands. He could rub horses—just touch one. He had such lovely, gentle horses. When he put on the bridle—most people always want to dominate the horse—he would just let that horse do it so nicely. All his horses were that type of a horse. The cows in the field—he knew every cow by its face. He had this wonderful gift. He could tell if a cow wasn't doing well.

We went over one day, and there he was cleaning a pheasant, just in front of us. He skinned it, opened it up and took out the insides. Really, it was a picture to watch him—watch those hands. He had the most wonderful hands, that man. And quiet hands. He just took the pheasant apart, and in two minutes it was all done. There was no mess, there was nothing. And that was his gift with those hands of his. You never saw him fly around with his hands. He always had that very quiet look, and his hands would be quiet.

One thing with Harry, he had the most wonderful eyes—wonderful eyes for people. He could tell what you were thinking.

EPILOGUE

Politics became for Harry Hays his life's ultimate fascination. Engaging work had always been for him mostly what life was really about—work and family and friends. And no work he did offered more absorbing challenges than politics because it covered the entire scope of human activities and interests. For Hays, I concluded from one of our last long conversations, his consummate political experience was co-chairing the joint Commons-Senate Constitution committee. From the beginning, his federal political career had been an Alberta farm boy's fascinated discovery of Canada from inside its pinnacle of power on Parliament Hill. His experience as co-chairman was a profound rounding-out of his discovery of the true nature of Canada and the true nature of Canadians' deepest personal interests. The experience permanently changed him in a fundamental way—the dimensions of Canadianism in his personal perception were irreversibly expanded.

But it was also an intensely exhausting experience that possibly contributed to his death; fully a year afterwards, he was still physically wearied.

Hays estimated that the committee had spent more time on the Charter of Rights than any other part of the Constitution package. "The Charter of Rights—that's what life's all about, isn't it?" He was convinced that the Trudeau charter was at least as good as and probably better than both the United Nations' Charter of Rights and Diefenbaker's Bill of Rights. "If every Canadian could sit down and read it and listen to what we listened to, I think that by and large they would agree that it's a pretty good Charter of Rights."

Of the Charter's critics, Hays said:

> To say Russia has a great charter of rights—well, you don't compare Canada and Russia at all. How can you make the Charter more made-in-Canada than it was? After all, we listened to the representatives of at least 24 million Canadians. We sat there for fifty-six days and we worked up until 11:30 at night, many, many nights, listening to Canadians. And all of these amendments were proposed by members of Parliament and by members of the government of Canada. So this Charter was made by Canadians in Canada.

At the conclusion of the joint committee's hearings on 4 March 1981, Hays presented to the Senate a final report on its activities. In doing so, he recalled that Chief James Gosnell of the Nishga Indian Tribal Council had pointed out that this was the first time ever that native peoples had been given an opportunity to express their views about their country's constitution. They had been ignored during the development of the British North America Act more than a century earlier. The point Hays made was that most other Canadians had also been ignored in the original making of Canada's Constitution. It had been written mostly in private meetings of legislators. "This," Hays said of his committee's lengthy hearings, "is the first opportunity for all Canadians to express themselves on their Constitution."

He was proud of the committee's work and its results. He pointed out that 131 members of the Commons and 51 senators altogether had participated in the committee's sessions. The committee had spent 176 hours listening to witnesses from the general public and 267 hours when time spent questioning federal ministers was included. This plus its private sessions arriving at its final report had consumed a total of 306 hours. Hays and his youthful co-chairman, Serge Joyal, had kept in mind his frequent advice that "down on my ranch we let them have a pretty loose rope." Altogether 107 amendments to the original federal government draft had been proposed to the committee, and it had accepted 66.

One of Hays's biggest disappointments, he said in his speech to the Senate, was that Premier Peter Lougheed of his home province of Alberta had declined to appear before the committee.

> As an Albertan, I am very sorry that Mr. Lougheed chose to ignore the committee. The people of Alberta deserved Mr. Lougheed's representations. Indeed, Mr. Lougheed had the obligation to represent before the committee the people who had elected him. . . . This was a committee which was trying to build a new, stronger Canada. There may be only two million Albertans, and two million Albertans do not constitute a large portion of the Canadian population, but I sincerely believe that their views, as expressed by their duly elected government, should have been presented.

Shortly before his death, Hays related how he had heard people from around the world say that there had never been so much input by so many people in a country that was forging its constitution. "Probably this one has had more public input than any other constitution of any country in the world. I don't know where else this happened. And it's the first one, you know, that has been put together without one shot being fired."

> There's something funny about Canadians. Maybe it's all over the world—that people tend to tear things down rather than try to make them better. That's more popular. When anybody decides he wants to do something, everybody wants to tear the scheme down.
>
> People hate change. It's like nylon stockings. When they made nylon stockings, it was ten years before women would wear them. Take the language rights in the Constitution. I can remember in 1963 and 1964, if you said to Albertans that you should have two languages, they'd run you out of town on a rail. But you know the last poll we took, 53 per cent of the people in Alberta think that you should have a second language. That took pretty near eighteen years, but finally they decided that a guy that could speak two languages was just a little bit better than one that could speak one language.
>
> Why are people so opposed to recognizing that all people are not equal and that you have to do a little for some that are less equal than others? I can't understand why people don't feel that way.

INDEX